THE DAILY EXPRESS
GUIDE TO FISHING

Alan Wrangles is a vastly experienced angler who
has written several books on the subject, as well as
contributing to angling magazines and appearing
frequently on radio. He lives in Cornwall.

THE DAILY EXPRESS GUIDE TO FISHING

Alan Wrangles

Illustrated by Brian Robertshaw

Star

A STAR BOOK

published by

the Paperback Division of
W. H. ALLEN & Co. Ltd

A Star Book
Published in 1982
by the Paperback Division of
W. H. Allen & Co. Ltd
A Howard and Wyndham Company
44 Hill Street, London W1X 8LB

Copyright © 1982 by Alan Wrangles
Illustrations copyright © 1982 by Brian Robertshaw

Reproduced, printed and bound in Great Britain by
Cox & Wyman Ltd, Reading

ISBN 0 352 30814 1

THE DAILY EXPRESS
GUIDE TO FISHING

Chapter 1

An introduction to the sport of angling

Angling is undoubtedly one of man's oldest sporting pas-
times but, curiously, it still remains in essence much as it has
always been – a fascinating contest between hunter and
hunted. However, over the centuries angling has gradually
become invested with a variety of laws and practices, and
anglers have grown steadily more specialised as the sport has
developed. Today there are three main groupings: coarse,
game and sea. Although individuals frequently take part in
more than one type or style of angling, it is essential to
appreciate that each has its own distinctive set of rules, of
which some are accepted as custom, whilst others are backed
by law.

Coarse angling
This is the art of catching freshwater fish other than salmon
and trout. The best known include barbel, bream, carp,
chub, dace, perch, pike and roach.

Inevitably the question is asked, 'Why *coarse* fish?' To the
best of my knowledge there is no generally accepted answer,
but most would agree that except for two or three species,
these fish make 'coarse' eating. Other characteristics of
coarse fish include the fact that they spawn in the spring, and
usually the eggs are laid on various water plants, but some
deposit their eggs in sheltered positions on the bottom. The
length of time taken for the eggs to hatch depends not only on
the species but also on variable factors such as water temperature. For example, perch eggs may take two or three weeks,

whereas bleak can hatch in about a week. During the spawning period coarse fish are, generally speaking, protected by the law. I say 'generally speaking' because there are certain exceptions which will be explained later.

The protection afforded to coarse fish during the spawning period is known as the 'close season', and its operation is clearly set out in the Salmon and Freshwater Fisheries Act 1975. Over the years, there has been a great deal of legislation affecting fishing. A number of bodies have also been responsible from time to time, for various functions relating to river management and water control, which in turn has had an effect, in one way or another, upon angling.

That is part of the historical aspect of the sport. Today, throughout England and Wales freshwater anglers are primarily concerned with the fishery bye-laws set out by the various Regional Water Authorities. These bye-laws incorporate the relevant sections of the Salmon and Freshwater Fisheries Act 1975. RWA bye-laws are designed to regulate the situations which occur within the area administered by the Authority. Some of the bye-laws deal specifically with coarse angling, others relate to salmon and trout fishing, and this includes net fishing for salmon and sea trout out to the six-mile limit, which is also controlled by RWA fishery bye-laws.

The angler is responsible for acquainting himself with the rules which apply to his area. Briefly, they are likely to cover points such as the purchase of a rod licence, prohibited ways of taking fish, and the periods during which it is illegal to fish – the close seasons.

A rod licence is issued for a set period, e.g. a day, week, or season, but it does no more than give the holder the right to fish with 'a rod and line'. It is not – and this is most important – a licence to fish in any stream or lake that lies within a particular RWA area. Permission to fish a certain stretch of water must be obtained separately. This aspect of coarse fishing is closely allied to club life. In the majority of cases, the close season for coarse fish is from March 15 to June 15, and includes both dates. However, there are exceptions. There is no close season for coarse fish in Devon and Corn-

2

wall, for example, and in some parts of England there are variations to the starting and ending dates.

The ten RWA covering England and Wales have a duty to care for and, where possible, improve the fisheries in their area. They all have officers responsible for fishery departments, and rod licence fees help to pay for this service. The RWA do much in the way of servicing and legislation, but most of the day-to-day administration and running of coarse fisheries is in the hands of angling clubs. These organisations are usually run on a voluntary basis, and memberships vary from a hundred or less, to a thousand or more.

Angling clubs are certainly not a modern development, although they have grown enormously in both size and importance during recent years. They probably have their origins within the orbit of competitive fishing, and there are references in many earlier books to anglers forming groups or clubs to compete for prizes. Big copper kettles were a favourite award in some northern areas a hundred or more years ago. Today, however, the town, works or village club is the cornerstone on which the whole fabric of coarse angling rests. The system is a simple one – the membership fees are used to pay the rent for an amount of fishable water – but there are also many highly complicated side issues.

Since good fisheries are in great demand, clubs do their best to arrange long-term leases with riparian owners and where possible clubs try to buy lakes or stretches of river bank. To give members additional facilities, individual clubs enter into a variety of agreements with other clubs or associations. Sometimes several organisations band together and combine their resources to rent or buy a coveted fishery. A club may also join an association to prevent others from outbidding them – or in some other way ousting them – on a water which they may hold on a rather tenuous rental agreement.

Club committees are faced with a hundred and one demands upon their time. Just consider the workload imposed by doing no more than collecting fees from several hundred members, issuing membership cards and paying various rentals. The sums involved may easily run into several thousands of pounds. Committees are also responsible for organising competitive events. Most clubs appoint Fishery Managers who work closely with the fisheries department of the local RWA. Working parties also have to be organised so that river and lake banks are kept in good order and in some cases the title Estate Manager would be more apt.

A town or village club may well belong to a county or regional organisation, which in turn is affiliated to the National Federation of Anglers. The NFA is the national body representing coarse anglers at the National Anglers Council, the sport's top organisation. Government turns to the NAC for any help or advice it may need on angling matters, and the NAC represents all shades of angling interests.

Although the bulk of coarse fisheries are controlled by clubs, there is also a not inconsiderable amount of 'commercial' water available to the angler. These range from those which are operated as a straightforward business venture, to fisheries which are designed to be financially self-supporting and no more. There are several organisations which run some of the best-known and most progressive fisheries in the former bracket, while one might look at some RWA operations for good examples of the latter. A well-run 'commercial' fishery can offer the 'occasional' angler all the facilities he requires. There is no individual involvement or responsibility, car parking and other necessary services are provided, and all the angler has to do is buy a permit. Frequently there are bailiffs or wardens to help and advise and, for many, 'commercial' fisheries are the complete answer.

The majority of coarse anglers, however, still prefer the sense of belonging which is part and parcel of being a club member. The easiest entrance to this world is through the tackle shop, or by referring to the local angling guide normally available from the RWA. These guides list water which is available locally, either on a day-permit basis or through club membership.

Water Authorities in England and Wales

North West Water Authority Rivers Division, PO Box 12, Warrington, Lancs.

Northumbrian Water Authority Northumbria House, Regent Centre, Gosforth, Newcastle upon Tyne, NE3 3PX.

Severn-Trent Water Authority Abelson House, 2297 Coventry Road, Sheldon, Birmingham, B26 3PU.

Yorkshire Water Authority West Riding House, 67 Albion Street, Leeds, LS1 5AA.

Anglian Water Authority Diploma House, Grammar School Walk, Huntingdon, PE18 6NZ.

Thames Water Authority Nugent House, Vastern Road, Reading, RG1 8DB.

Southern Water Authority Guildbourne House, Worthing, Sussex, BN11 1LD.

Wessex Water Authority Wessex House, Passage Street, Bristol, BS2 0JQ.

South West Water Authority 3/5 Barnfield Road, Exeter, Devon, EX1 1RE.

Welsh Water Authority Cambrian Way, Brecon, Powys, LD3 7HP.

All RWA issue angling guides or similar publications. Some issue these free, others make a charge; when writing for information always include a stamped self addressed envelope. A list of organisations who can also supply further information is given below. Once again, when writing for help always include a self addressed stamped envelope.

Automobile Association Trade Sales Dept., Fanum House, Basingstoke, Hants, RG21 2BN.
(AA Guide to Angling in Great Britain)
Northern Ireland, Department of Agriculture for Dundonald House, Upper Newtownards Road, Belfast, BT4 3SB.
Irish Tourist Board Bord Failte, Baggot Street Bridge, Dublin, 2.

Scottish Tourist Board 23 Ravelston Terrace, Edinburgh, EH4 3EU.

Peak National Park Office, Information Group, Park Office, Aldern House, Baslow Road, Bakewell, DE4 1AE.

Central Electricity Generating Board (North Western Region) Bron Heulog, Conwy Road, Llandudno Junction, Gwynedd, LL31 9TQ.

National Anglers' Council 11 Cowgate, Peterborough, PE1 1LR.

Areas in England within Welsh area.

Areas in Wales within Severn-Trent area.

1 . North-East
2 . North-West
3 . Yorkshire
4 . Welsh
5 . Severn-Trent
6 . Anglian
7 . Thames
8 . South-West
9 . Wessex
10 . Southern

So far I have deliberately avoided mentioning Scotland and Ireland, as things are quite different there. Coarse fishing is, for the most part, free in Scotland. Free, that is, just so long as you have the riparian owner's permission. North of the border the local angler is traditionally a salmon or trout man, and only in recent years has there been any great interest in coarse fishing. In both Ulster and Eire there is a vast amount of coarse fishing which is either freely available or extremely cheap. In Chapter 6 there is further information about coarse fishing and licences in Scotland and Ireland.

Game fishing

The salmon and its relatives are both valuable and much sought after fish, so it is understandable that fishing for them is relatively expensive. Also, because they need rather special environmental conditions, they are less widely distributed than coarse fish. However, in recent years trout fishing has become more readily available through the practice of stocking reservoirs and opening them to the public on a fee-paying basis.

The members of the salmon family with which we are concerned include the salmon itself, migratory or sea trout, brown and rainbow trout. Grayling are a member of this family but because they are a spring spawning variety, they are generally classed as coarse fish.

Both salmon and migratory or sea trout are born in fresh water, but they move out to sea for a period before returning to the stream of their birth, or, in the case of the sea trout, to a suitable fresh water environment where they spawn and start the cycle. As they come back into esturial waters they can face the first of many obstacles – professional fishermen. Once past this hazard the fish then face a journey upstream where anglers will try to take them in a variety of ways, frequently on an artificial fly. The methods of fishing are frequently controlled by RWA bye-laws. For example, one of the regulations relating to the Axe district of South West Water Authority states: 'No person shall use in fishing with rod and line for salmon in this district any shrimp, prawn, worm or maggot, whether real or imitation, as bait.' Fishery owners may also place certain limitations on the methods which can be used. Restrictions of a similar nature may also apply to trout fishing in different parts of England and Wales.

It is absolutely essential for the newcomer to angling to realise that salmon fishing is a well controlled activity and is generally far more expensive than coarse fishing. The expense is not so much a matter of more costly tackle as a reflection of the sheer economic value of the salmon. To a lesser extent, this rule also applies to trout fishing.

As game fish are autumn and winter spawning fish, the close season is set to suit the species. Generally speaking the close season for trout extends from about the end of September or mid-October until mid-March or the beginning of April. There are slight variations according to the situations prevailing in different RWA areas. With salmon angling there can be quite wide gaps between the close seasons as they apply to river systems, even within a single RWA area. For example, on the river Teign the close season begins on August 31, opening again for salmon angling on the following February 1. The River Camel, on the other hand, closes on December 15, to re-open the following April 1, but it is important to realise that as a result of conservation measures and other considerations, all these dates are subject to change.

The wide variations occur because of the differences in the timing of the arrival of migratory fish in the rivers. Close seasons for migratory trout also vary, but not usually to the same extent as salmon.

To summarise briefly: game fishing can be placed under three main headings, (1) salmon (2) migratory and (3) non-migratory trout. Salmon fishing is a river sport which, generally speaking, is expensive since the actual cost is related to the quality of the sport. It is strictly controlled, with most of the best stretches of the finest rivers in private hands, and access is very limited. There are, however, many hotels and riverside inns which offer good salmon angling facilities to both guests and day visitors. RWA guide books are an invaluable source of further information. In some areas local

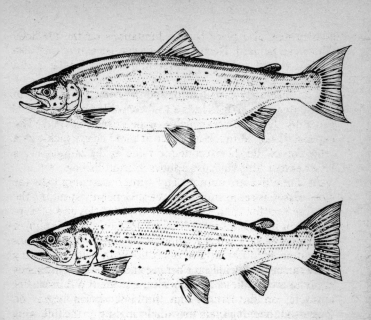

Top: salmon. Above: migratory or sea trout.

clubs and associations offer the occasional day ticket and, once again, RWA guides can help considerably. The complete novice would do well to spend a few days or a week at a hotel specialising in salmon fishing holidays. These frequently have 'ghillies' available, and a few days spent with one of these 'professionals' of the salmon fishing world can provide an education that will last an angling lifetime.

Similar comments can be made about sea trout fishing, but here the situation is slightly easier as sea trout rivers are more plentiful. For example, most rivers in Sussex have a run of sea trout, but certainly no salmon. Once again, consult your RWA guide. Trout fishing is now widely available, and throughout England and Wales it can be enjoyed for quite modest fees.

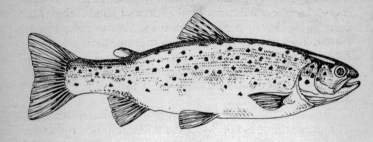

Brown trout.

The majority of people in England and Wales are within 30 miles of a reasonable trout angling centre. Many public water supply reservoirs offer top-class sport. They are kept well stocked and the facilities provided frequently include not only car parks, but also a well equipped anglers' lodge as well as a store with limited tackle supplies. Charges for this type of angling are often no more than double or treble what might be asked for similar coarse angling facilities. Reservoirs are normally stocked with both brown and rainbow trout, but rainbow trout predominate.

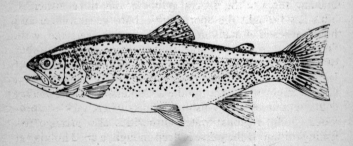

Rainbow trout.

In Scotland the salmon is king, and the waters holding them are jealously guarded. A large number of hotels offer superb facilities, and many local associations and clubs issue permits for limited periods to visitors. Scotland also offers extensive sea trout angling on much the same basis as salmon fishing. Trout fishing is generally free, just as long as the angler has the landowner's consent. Both Northern and Southern Ireland offer excellent game fishing, and further details are in Chapter 6.

This, then, is the general picture of freshwater angling. Throughout England or Wales the RWA and their bye-laws are the main things to look at and it is essential to both understand and abide by the regulations. Always remember that, in England and Wales, rod licences are obligatory, and these have an increasing scale of charges. For example, a course angling rod licence may be £1–£1.50, trout (including migratory and rainbow trout) £4.00–£6.00 per season while a rod licence for salmon fishing could be £17.00 or more. These charges vary from area to area, and the greater licence always covers the lesser. Access to coarse angling water and the general activities associated with the sport are best achieved through a club (see local RWA angling guide). Those not so interested in personal involvement should consider the facilities offered by commercial fisheries.

In summarising the initial considerations of game fishing, the first conclusion must be that trout angling has been given an enormous boost by the practice of stocking reservoirs and opening them to the general public as day-ticket fisheries. This has brought the sport within both geographical and financial reach of many millions who, a few years ago, were far removed from reasonable trout facilities. A large number of newcomers to fly fishing will enter the sport as a result of learning to cast and handle a fish at one of these waters. Others might well elect to take a weekend or whole week's course at one of the fly-fishing schools where tackle is provided. Some regional water authorities also arrange fly-fishing tuition. If the purse is deep enough, a good holiday at a specialist hotel, plus the individual attention of a first-class 'ghillie' will set you up for a sporting lifetime.

Sea angling

This sport divides quite naturally into boat and shore fishing, but obviously there are a number of sub-divisions under each. The majority of sea anglers fish from the shore, and in this I include piers, jetties, harbour walls and rocks. Except where there are restrictions, such as those imposed by harbour authorities and the Ministry of Defence, sea fishing is free. Naturally, most pier owners or lessees make a charge, but this is for the facility not the actual fishing.

There is an incredibly wide variety of fish in the seas around the British Isles, ranging from heavy-weights such as 200lb halibut, 500lb mako shark and 100lb conger eel, to the more ordinary 2lb plaice and flounder. In between these two extremes there are many species which give both sporting and gastronomic delight. For example, beach anglers catch bass, cod, mullet, sole, dab and, on occasions, mackerel by the dozen. Although boat anglers frequently strike into a much wider selection of fish, including pollack, ling, ray, dogfish and turbot, they are more likely to be affected by 'dirty' weather conditions.

One of the great joys of sea angling is that it is possible to 'have a go' on a shoestring budget. The novice can try deep-water fishing for no more than the price of a seat on board a charter boat. These craft operate from many ports around the coast, and the skippers are, in the main, very helpful sportsmen who will even loan the beginner suitable tackle. (See Chapter 6 for more detailed advice.)

Pier fishing can be an even cheaper exercise for the novice. One can sometimes hire equipment by the day from tackle kiosks on piers, but where these facilities do not exist, try a simple handline, the cost of which is negligible. For the beginner, handline fishing can be a lot of fun, and can be used from both piers and boats. In fact many really keen rod-and-line anglers started out with no more than a handline dangled over the stern of a boat. After they had got the feel of things, they soon graduated to rod and reel.

Straightforward beach fishing involves the art of casting terminal tackle and bait possibly a hundred yards or more. This feat is not accomplished without suitable equipment

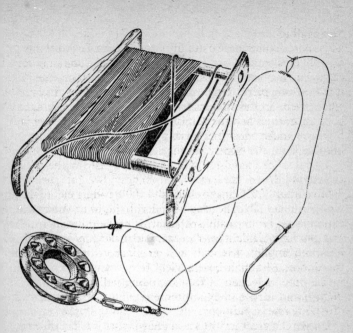

Hand line.

and a high degree of skill. However, it does not call for a vast amount of physical strength, a fact to which many ladies will testify. Efficient beach casting tackle is not cheap, but neither need it cost the earth. Before becoming committed to spending a fair sum of money, a trial or two with a competent angler is the best way of coming to terms with a unique sporting recreation.

There cannot be many who suddenly decide that beach fishing is the sport for them. The attraction must surely occur as a result of watching anglers either taking part in a competition or just fishing for the sheer fun of it. Others are probably interested by friends who are keen, in which case the necessary tuition will already be near to hand. For the others, the best introduction is undoubtedly through club membership. Sea angling clubs are legion throughout the British Isles.

Most clubs belong to larger associations which may have a regional or national basis, and overall there is the National Anglers Council. (Addresses of sea angling organisations appear in Chapter 6.) Generally speaking sea angling club fees are less than freshwater organisations', but they have much to offer the new entrant to the sport. It is by fishing as a club member that one learns about such things as where and when to fish and which baits bring the best results in particular locations. In short, the novice can learn to be an angler.

Safety
Most of us face a variety of risks every day – but there is little point in adding to the danger by acting stupidly whilst taking part in a sport or pastime. Apart from the fact that anglers are on or near water, there are particular dangers involved in certain angling practices and these are explained in the appropriate sections. Here I will do no more than point out that only fools and the very inexperienced go afloat without the necessary life-saving equipment. Ponds and streams also offer a variety of hazards which can kill the unwary. Remember to tread softly and carefully – it pays in the end.

Insurance
Some insurance companies offer specialised angling policies. These cover not only your personal equipment, but also offer third-party cover. Clubs frequently give their members cover as an extra benefit, but consider for a moment the problems one might face if a cast went astray, and the hooks struck a passer-by.

Courtesy
Angling, in common with most other sports and games, has a number of unwritten laws which, when followed, improve the day for everyone. An angler fishing from a stance sheltered by a tree or bush will not thank you for standing on the sky-line and walking about as you shout: 'Caught anything.' The angler facing you from the opposite bank will not be made happy by your great clods of groundbait disturbing the stream for yards around, and the landowner can do without

14

your leaving gates open, dropping litter or breaking through his hedges.

A stretch of salmon fishing is often divided into what are called 'beats'. It sometimes happens that anglers are allocated 'beats' on a time basis, with a change-over at mid-day. A sportsman is one who leaves his beat with some time to spare, and with as little bankside commotion as possible. He would also be respected if he walked to his next beat by following a path well away from the bank.

Generally speaking, all these unwritten laws are little more than common sense and good manners. If you always 'fish as you would be fished by', you will not go far wrong.

Chapter 2

About tackle and basic methods

The vast and seemingly complicated array of tackle displayed by most dealers has not arrived on the scene by accident. Of course, certain items might be considered more ornamental than useful, but these are in the minority. Most equipment has been designed to help the angler overcome the many problems posed by both fish and environment, the two things that decide the type of equipment you need. Roach and dace fishing, for example, calls for entirely different tackle to that which would be used when spinning for pike or casting from a beach for bass. So before choosing equipment, the angler should have a basic knowledge of both the conditions and the species which it will be called upon to match.

Fortunately this is not as complicated as it sounds, as there is not only a well-defined line between freshwater and sea angling, but the divisions within these two main persuasions are quite easily made. At the moment the market is dominated by the modern, tough and highly-efficient hollow glass rod. These are constructed by wrapping resin-coated woven glass cloth around a mandrel – a steel rod which sets the shape. The material is then heat-cured in an oven, and the resulting 'tube' is called a 'blank'. The rod's ultimate strength and the way it acts when under stress is determined by its design. The important factors are wall thickness, overall length and taper. By varying these dimensions the designer can create either a wand-like blank which, when fitted with hand grip, reel fitting and rings, will be suited to casting feather-light float tackle on a gossamer-thin line, or a greatly beefed-up version which is capable of withstanding the shock of casting 8oz of lead 100 yards or more out to sea.

Hollow glass blanks make fine rods which are light yet powerful, and both sensitive and extremely versatile, but they are not as cheap to produce as 'solid glass' rods which have a smaller, yet significant share of the market. The term 'solid glass' is used to describe a blank which is made by setting glass fibres into resin. The fibres are laid longitudinally, and the strength – and to some extent the final price – is determined by the amount of fibre used. A high proportion of glass-fibre-to-resin results in a stronger, but usually more expensive, blank.

Naturally, this is not the only consideration. Fittings, such as the rings and handle, all have a great bearing on the final cost, but it can be safely assumed that a good manufacturer would not place poor quality fittings onto a high-grade blank. The tackle trade is extremely competitive, and my experience is that both quality and price are very closely linked.

There are other methods of building rods, apart from hollow and solid glass which dominate the market. Cane rods are still made, and without doubt they can be a joy to use, although poor quality soft cane defies description. Carbon fibre is said by some to be the material of the future, and indeed there is already a quite substantial move in this direction particularly in the fly fishing range where it has made remarkable progress. It is an expensive material, however, and many would argue that its advantages do not justify the quite significant extra cost. Time alone will tell.

However, a lot of development has taken place over the past few years, and manufacturers are constantly striving to produce new ideas and designs. Currently, in the glass and carbon range there are rods made of carbon, glass and mixed carbon and glass cloths, and also various resin systems are used to bond these materials. Even a metal derivative is now being added in an effort to gain even more power.

Rod making has, in the main, long since departed the 'hand craft' era, and nowadays some manufacturers talk about computer technology. But basically, all the leading manufacturers offer a good range of exceptionally well produced rods, and in the final analysis, you get what you pay for. However, there is such fierce competition throughout the whole of the fishing tackle trade that the buyer can be reasonably assured of getting value for money. Having settled on the type of rod, the buyer really only has to decide which particular model suits his pocket and personal preference.

Many fly fishers of very long standing argue quite forcibly that good cane is the only material that makes a sweet-actioned fly rod. But at this point we start entering the realms of personal choice and opinion, two creative lines of thought which most anglers seem to develop quite rapidly.

Freshwater and sea angling rods have certain common features. They must all be equipped with handles and a fitting with which to secure a reel. Rings to guide the line and transfer the strain from line to rod must also be fitted. These are placed at intervals along the blank, which, for the sake of convenience, must be broken into two or more sections. A variety of materials are used for rod handles. Cork is an old favourite, and is certainly very efficient, but so are many of the newer man-made materials which are placed on a wide range of rods, from light fly-casting wands to massively powerful deep-sea rods.

It can be accepted that a good standard rod from a reputable maker will be equipped with a handle which will be perfectly adequate. However, you may not like the feel of a particular substance and this is where personal preference is an important factor. The choice of a different handle material is very wide, even within a certain division, so never buy a piece of equipment as fundamental as a rod unless you are totally satisfied in all respects.

Reel fittings are extremely important, as they not only lock your reel tightly onto the rod, but they also hold the reel in a position which should be comfortable when in use. Coarse angling float fishing or bottom rods are best served by what are called 'sliding' winch, or reel fittings. These can be set at any point on the handle and will hold the reel surprisingly firmly.

Various manufacturers have developed their own special-

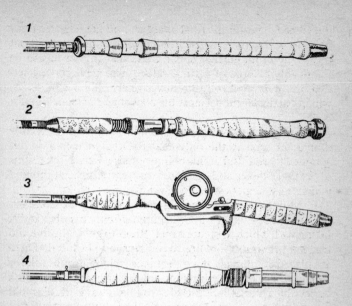

1. Sliding fittings. 2. Screw fittings. 3. Offset rod handle with a multiplier in the 'on top' position. 4. Screw lock fitting at the end of a fly rod.

ised reel fittings, and in some cases these will only accept a limited range of reels – possibly just those from the same company. This is an important point to check when buying a rod. Make sure that your reel is a perfect match, for if it twists whilst playing a fish you will find it almost impossible to operate it correctly. Fly rods are designed to hold the reel at the butt end of the handle, as fly casting techniques are a completely different skill and the reel needs to be placed low down on the rod.

Rings are more than just twists of metal used to keep the line tidy between the reel and rod tip. In the case of a bottom rod, they should hold the light line away from the rod because in wet conditions the line will tend to cling to it, decreasing casting efficiency, and affecting both accuracy and distance.

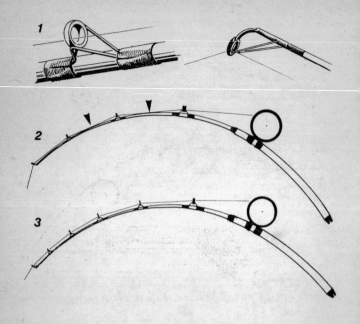

1. Stand off rod ring and end ring. 2. Insufficient rings or incorrectly spaced rings may cause friction against the rod. 3. Extra rings correctly spaced will prevent friction.

It is also vital for the rod to have the correct number of rings. Too few and there is uneven strain which will almost certainly result in tackle failure. As pressure is being concentrated at one spot instead of being evenly distributed, either the line or the rod will break long before its maximum strength is utilised.

If a rod is designed to be fished with a reel in the 'on top' position, the rings must be spaced so that when a strain is imposed, the line is still kept above, yet following the rod's curve.

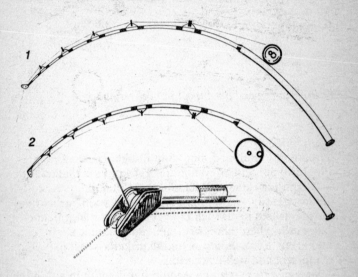

1. Rod under strain with reel in 'on top' position. 2. Centre-pin reel 'under' the rod. Inset: double roller end ring.

Sea angling rods designed for boat fishing are sometimes equipped with double-roller end rings which allow the rod to accept both a multiplier and a reel (for example a heavy duty centre-pin) designed to be fished 'under' the rod. The problems created by a spiralling line as it spills from a fixed spool reel are minimised by the provision of a large diameter butt ring. This accepts and channels the line which might twist around and snag on a smaller diameter ring. A large ring also minimises friction.

Fortunately, quality rods from reputable manufacturers

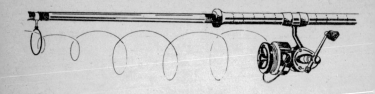

Large butt ring and fixed spool reel delivering line.

are correctly equipped, but with fittings representing possibly thirty per cent or even more of the rod's manufacturing
price, this is an area in which some will attempt to save costs.
In short, sturdy, well-finished reel fittings, good quality rings
and specialised items such as double-roller or large diameter
butt rings where necessary, are not manufacturers' gim-
micks, but are an indication of the maker's desire to present
an efficient and well-equipped rod.

Similar remarks can be made about the way in which the
rod sections are joined. Normally, they break down into two
or three sections, as it is impracticable to store or travel
around with one-piece, 10 or 12ft 'poles'. There are
specialised exceptions to this general rule. For example,
some expert casters who compete in tournaments and give
exhibitions may build their own one-piece rods, and a few
who have the necessary facilities may fish with similar
equipment. However, the vast majority use the standard
items which break down into sections, and for many years the
stiffening created by metal sockets and ferrules was an
impediment which has now been largely overcome by the
development of rods which are called 'ferruless'. The majority of hollow glass rods are now constructed so that each
section terminates with the appropriate joint. The blank is
fashioned so that both the socket and ferrule are of the same
material and are part of the blank.

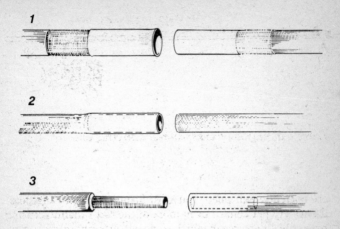

*1. Brass socket and ferrule joint. 2. Ferruless joint. 3. Spigotted
ferruless rod joint.*

Another development is the spigotted ferruless rod. The
spigott protrudes from the lower section and is inserted into
the upper – a system opposite to the traditional way – as
illustrated by the diagram of the brass socket and ferrule
joint.

Designers have done much in recent years to improve both
the casting and fish-playing attributes of the various types of
rods. They have been greatly helped by the tremendously
strong and versatile material at their command, but to have
taken such enormous advantage of its properties is to their
credit. Basically, rods have either what is called 'tip' action or
'through' action, and designers create these features by varying the taper and wall thickness. Although it is not possible to
give a solid glass rod the same degree of sensitivity as its
hollow glass counterpart, there are certain areas in which
solid rods perform quite adequately, and probably some boat
fishing rods are the best examples of this fact.

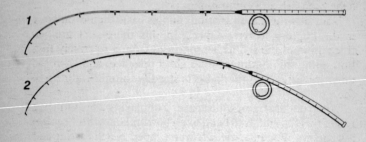

1. Tip action rod under strain. 2. Through action rod under strain.

The inevitable question is: 'Which is the best, a "tip" or "through" action rod?' My comment at the beginning of this chapter, that most equipment has been designed to help the angler overcome the many problems posed by both fish and environment, is well illustrated by the rod maker's art. Neither 'tip' nor 'through' action is superior, except for performing the particular task for which it was designed. 'Tip' action is created by a fast taper – a rod which is thick at the butt end and, tapering rapidly, produces a slim tip – and the action can be highlighted by hanging a weight onto the tip. It will be seen that the bend occurs at this end while the handle and section immediately above remain virtually straight. As the weight is increased, so the point at which the curve starts progresses down the rod.

The 'slow' taper or 'through' action rod, on the other hand, has not only a thinner butt end, but also a thicker tip. In other words, a slower or more gradual taper from butt to tip. A similar weight or strain test shows quite clearly that the rod's action is very different. A smooth curve will develop, starting just above the handle and continuing through to the tip. These two basic design features are carried by rods throughout the whole range, so that a particular situation can be met by a rod suited to match or counter whatever problems both fish and environment pose.

Naturally there are variations on this basic theme, and one is the popular 'reverse taper'. In this there is a gradual thickening of the rod as it progresses from a relatively thin butt end. This continues for a short distance, and then the taper 'reverses' and the rod gets steadily thinner right up to the tip.

When under strain, whilst casting or playing a heavy fish, a rod of this type tends to bend like a bow and does offer certain advantages. For example, a 'reverse taper' beach casting rod is perfectly matched to the 'lay-back' style of casting. Also, in my opinion, they are the easiest type to use whilst mastering the art of beach fishing. The softer, smoother action is an advantage, I believe, whilst casting baits, such as peeler crab, which can so easily be torn from the hook by a snatching, jerky casting movement.

Before considering the various types of rod (spinning, bottom fishing, boat and so on) in greater detail, it is important to note the relationship between rod, line and reel, an affiliation referred to as 'balance'. Manufacturers build both rods and reels for specific purposes and, despite the fact that this message is hammered home time and time again, it is a truth which is frequently ignored. A rod designed to float fish for roach and dace cannot become a substitute for a rod intended to cast perhaps 70g and hold a 10lb barbel in a fast-running stream. There are those who think that this can be done by just using a much heavier line but nothing could be further from fact.

Each and every rod is designed to operate within a fairly narrow band of line strengths, so always remember that it is equally wrong to use a line which is either too strong or too weak. One which is more powerful than it should be can break the rod, while at the other extreme the line will be snapped time after time. It is also important to choose a reel which relates not only to the rod and line, but also to the style of fishing. A reel which is designed to hold, for example, 100m of 3lb breaking strain (BS) line, would be totally unsuited to being filled with 20lb BS line. Not only would there be an insufficient amount of line to fish correctly, but the whole rod-line-reel strength relationship would be destroyed. Absorb these fundamental points and the finer points will rapidly fall into place.

Coarse fishing rods

Within this range there are bottom rods, which are general-purpose float fishing 'poles' between approximately 10 and 14ft long, leger rods, which are shorter and more powerful, and spinning rods that vary from 10-ft items designed to be held with both hands while casting lures weighing up to 70gm to ultra-light 6ft wands which are matched to casting no more than 15gm.

A rod designed for float fishing must have extra length so that line can be picked up rapidly when striking at a fish which has taken the bait possibly 30 yards or more downstream of the point from which you are casting. Tackle control is also easier with a rod of adequate length, for example when the float is being carried by the stream, or when fishing deep water.

Leger rods do not need the additional length as the style of fishing for which they are designed involves casting basically heavier terminal tackle to a specific target area. There it will either remain stationary on the bottom, or it will be rolled along by the current.

At the time of writing the British record for a rod-caught carp stands at 44lb and the barbel record is 13lb 12oz. Both these species are strong creatures, and to their natural power one must add the underwater hazards which the angler faces when hunting them. Carp thrive in still waters providing ample plant cover. The angler must therefore contend not only with a heavyweight adversary, but also a mass of natural hazards. Barbel are also strong creatures and although they do not reach the size of carp, their natural habitat – weir pools and rivers with a strong flow – more than compensates for their lower poundage.

These details highlight, once again, those two vital considerations – fish and environment. It cannot be overstated how important it is to equate your equipment with those two factors. For example if an angler were fishing still waters, canals and slow-flowing rivers up to 10ft deep which hold reasonable stocks of species such as dace, roach, perch, chub and bream, then he would be well served by an 8oz hollow glass 12ft rod lined with a 4–5lb BS monofilament. Ideally, a leger rod should be equipped with a top ring which incorporates a socket into which either a 'swing' or 'quiver' tip can be screwed. These 'bite' detecting devices are highly flexible extra tips which react instantly to the pull of a fish. As they offer little resistance, a 'taking fish' is not deterred.

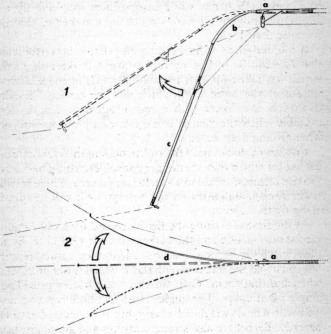

1. a. End ring with threaded socket. b. Flexible connector. c. Glass fibre hollow or solid section. Depending on the take, the section may lift or drop. 2. a. End ring with threaded socket. b. Flexible hollow or solid section.

Certain items such as match rods and roach poles have been developed to cater for the specialised needs of the devotees of competitive or match fishing. While they are beautifully proportioned and highly efficient items of equipment, they are in a class of their own, and outside the scope of this book. However, one collection of specialised rods are extremely important to the angler who wants to get on level terms with the larger of our freshwater species. These are rods developed by and for the hunters of specimen-sized carp and barbel. Here the angler may have to contend with fish of far more than average size and power. As soon as heavier species are introduced, then a somewhat 'beefed-up' rod and stronger line must be considered. Deeper water might well call for a longer rod, particularly if small fish such as roach and dace are predominant. For this style of angling, a lightish rod combining a very firm tip action would be ideal. Of course, a variety of techniques can always be employed to enhance whatever advantages your tackle gives, but this subject is developed later in this chapter.

Spinning rods come in a profusion of lengths, and display a wide range of attributes. Once again, match equipment against quarry and conditions. Big baits cast into deep water for large pike means using a much heavier and longer rod than one would select if fishing perch in a 4ft-deep stream. However, for most general purposes, rods between 6 and 8ft long, and designed to cast weights ranging from around 15 to 30gm should cover most situations.

Coarse angling reels

The vast majority of coarse anglers operate a fixed spool reel for all the various styles of fishing. Without doubt it is an extremely versatile piece of equipment, but some, a dwindling minority of whom I am one, still prefer to use a centre-pin for certain methods.

A fixed spool reel is a most efficient item and, if used correctly, long and relatively accurate casting can be achieved with no more than a few hours' practice.

First, something about the reel. When delivering line, the

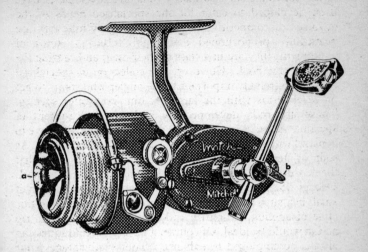

*Fixed spool reel (Mitchell Match). a. Tension control.
b. Ratchet.*

spool remains stationary. The weight of the tackle flying towards its target draws the required amount and, as the terminal tackle reaches its destination, line ceases to flow. This fact reduces to a minimum the chances of the line tangling and knotting. Line is regained by operating the crank handle which is linked to the bale arm. The arm closes automatically as the handle is turned, and the internal mechanism operates both the spool, in a reciprocating action, and the bale arm. As the spool moves to and fro the bale arm goes around, re-laying the line evenly onto the spool.

The spool is designed to turn and yield line in a controlled manner as it reacts to the strain imposed by a large fish. The point at which the spool begins to revolve automatically is governed by the amount of pressure exerted by the tension control nut as it presses the spool against friction plates. When set correctly, the spool should begin to give line as the rod tip is pulled over to a point at right angles to the butt. If the tension is incorrectly set, either the tackle will fail, or it becomes impossible to play the fish properly. Set the tension as soon as the line has been layed through the rod rings. Hold the running end of the line in one hand and the rod handle in the other. Hold the line firm and exert strain on the rod tip. Adjust the tension nut so that line is given automatically as the tip comes over to an angle between 45 and 60 degrees. Do not fix hooks and weights before checking the tension – this is how accidents happen. If, while actually playing a fish, a small amount of extra tension is needed, place a forefinger onto the spool. Never tighten the control nut.

At this point it can be appreciated that a fixed spool reel is a highly ingenious piece of equipment and, in general, reels with similar features must have comparable mechanisms. In fact, with competiton at the level it is, you can be assured that all reels within a particular price range would be similar, with better quality being matched by higher prices. Most reels of this type have similar external features and even the internal mechanisms may look alike. However, when choosing a reel I would be looking for one from a manufacturer who machined the gears from solid pieces of hard metal and used a hard metal face against which to run bearings. Considering the vast amount of wear given to the line guide on the bale arm, nothing less than a finely machined roller would give maximum service.

When choosing any type of reel, you will find price a very fair guide to both quality and the length of service you can reasonably expect it to give. At the same time, do not overlook the question of service and spares, as this can be extremely important. A reel that can, if necessary, be repaired by a specialist tackle dealer is an item well worth considering, not least because it avoids heavy postal charges.

Both 'push-button' and 'closed face' fixed spool reels are extremely popular. The 'push-button' type has a very fast line pick-up, and is a favourite with match or competitive anglers. It is a very sophisticated item, particularly suited to angling with light tackle and, as the spool is protected against

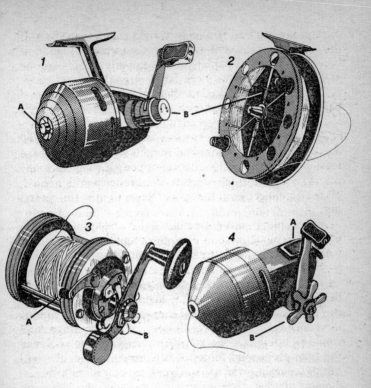

1. Push-button reel. 2. Centre-pin. 3. Multiplier. 4. Closed-face.
A. Line release control. B. Line tension control.

rain, it is an aid to casting with a fine line. The 'closed-face' reel is designed to be fished in the 'on-top' position. It is an ideal reel for spinning or casting plugs and similar lures.

The term 'multiplier' is used as a blanket description to cover a number of wide-frame reels. They are more usually associated with sea angling, but the freshwater models are popular with many who spin for species such as pike and salmon, and especially so where conditions call for the use of line around 20lb BS. These reels have a gear system which drives the spool at a faster rate than the crank-handle is turned and a ratio of 4:1 is quite usual. As this type of reel delivers line from a revolving reel there is considerably less frictional loss when heavier lines are used.

On a fixed spool reel the distance between the spool's lip and the top of the stored line increases quite rapidly during a cast. As this gap widens the frictional loss builds up as the line is pulled over the lip. Although this is a minimal problem when very light tackle is being used, it becomes an important factor when lines of around 20lb BS or more are concerned. In short, the multipliers revolving drum delivers line with as little frictional loss at the end of a cast as at the beginning, whereas friction steadily increases as each additional metre of line is pulled from a fixed spool reel.

There are few, if any, definite advantages in using a centre-pin reel, and probably the majority of present-day anglers do not own one. However, being able to use a centre-pin gives some personal satisfaction as it produces a high degree of casting accuracy and tackle control. By pulling a measured length of line from the reel it is possible to cast to the same spot time and time again, and there is also pleasure to be had in playing a fish directly, instead of having all one's mistakes countered automatically by the ingenious devices built into the reel by the designer.

Line

Nylon monofilament line dominates both salt and freshwater angling and is, in fact, the only material which can be satis-factorily used in conjunction with a fixed spool reel. It is widely available, relatively cheap, and comes in various strengths which are measured and assessed either as a 'break-ing strain' (BS) or a 'test rating'. Generally, line is tested when wet, and those classified by BS will not, when in good condition, snap until a steady strain exceeding their rating has been exerted. A 4lb BS line, for example, would probably stand up to 4.5 or even 5lb strain before snapping. On the other hand, a line with a test rating will break as its stated strength is approached. Test rating is particularly important in sea angling, as all world records recognised by the International Game Fish Association are listed under headings denoting test ratings.

Nylon line is supplied in a variety of colours and shades. A number of claims about colour have been made but after many years of fishing with lines of various hues I have not been able to detect any great advantages between the colours and surface finishes, apart from a polished or matt surface. When fishing in shallow, clear water under bright conditions I prefer a matt finished line, otherwise I would use a polished line because, generally speaking, size for size they tend to be just that much stronger. It is also important, all other factors permitting, to select a line with the least diameter in relation to its strength. By using such a line, drag imposed by tide and current is cut to a minimum, and spool capacity is increased; sometimes quite dramatically. Some mono lines possess what I would call an excess of elasticity, and this is not a particularly good feature as it can cushion the strike, and so prevent the hook from being driven home.

It is essential that only those knots designed for use with nylon be used when assembling tackle. Even these can reduce the line's effective strength by as much as 25 per cent. An incorrect knot could possibly halve its strength, or even pull undone when subjected to strain. The leading brands offer line which is reliable and up to a high standard, but each has its own characteristics. Personal preference will be the final arbiter, but know why you are making a particular choice. Is it colour, surface finish, or has the line just the right degree of 'spring' or possibly you favour a line which is more limp than others? Be aware of the various qualities, and use them to your advantage.

Despite the fact that nylon monofilament is a very tough commodity, it is frequently damaged, and often without the angler realising just how badly until it snaps while playing 'the fish of a lifetime'. Line is damaged in a number of ways, such as from excessive strain, degeneration due to long exposure to sunlight, or abrasion caused by anything, from rubbing against an underwater obstruction to the damage which is done by a faulty rod ring or line guide. Incorrect knots also contribute greatly to line failure.

Excessive strain distorts the line's molecular pattern, but being left completely loose for an hour or so will frequently be sufficient for complete recuperation. However, if a well stretched line is laid back onto a reel, it is more than possible that the spool will be completely distorted by the crushing effect of the line as it re-establishes itself. This is probably the biggest single cause of reel damage. I have seen a reel virtually reduced to its component parts by the crushing power of nylon monofilament.

Strong sunlight over a long period weakens mono line so it should always be stored in a cool, dark and dry place. But, of course, do not discount the hours it may have been exposed to this damaging element during a season's use. A high proportion of a line's total strength is contained in its outer layer, so it is particularly vulnerable to damage by abrasion.

Learn to tie, and always use knots designed for nylon monofilament as those developed for use with multi-strand line are just not suitable. Make a habit of changing your line at the end of each season, and completely reverse it half-way through. If any damage is detected, replace your line immediately as it is pointless to continue using a line which will almost certainly fail just at the moment you hope it will hold.

Although the majority of sea anglers use nylon monofilament, there are times when it is far better to use a braided line such as sea dacron. Although more expensive, braided line has one big feature which is most important under some circumstances – it does not stretch. This means it can be relied on to set a hook more firmly, which can be a vital factor when fishing in deep water and using possibly 8oz or more of lead. Under these circumstances nylon monofilament can stretch to such an extent that although the rod tip has been moved five or six feet, the hook does no more than twitch sluggishly as all the movement at one end is absorbed by the line's elasticity.

Braided lines of around 20 BS are sometimes used when spinning for salmon, and particularly so in a turbulent and strong-flowing river. A braided line's lack of 'stretch' also enables a 'bite' to be felt more accurately. The various 'hap-

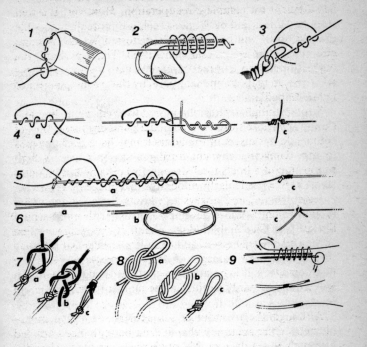

1. *spool knot,* 2. *hook snood,* 3. *double clinch knot,* 4. *blood knot,* 5. *shock leader knot,* 6. *dropper knot,* 7. *tucked sheet bend,* 8. *double overhead loop knot,* 9. *backing nail knot.*

penings' at the business end of the tackle are transmitted by the line and, with growing experience, the angler finds that it is possible to understand the strange language coming from below. This is not meant to imply that only braided line gives a satisfaction of this kind – but it does do it more efficiently under these particular circumstances.

Hooks

It frequently amazes me that an item seemingly as simple as a fish hook could have become as complicated as it has. Over the years a multiplicity of shapes and even colours have been designed and produced and it is possible to find four or more variations of one particular shape.

During the hundreds of years hooks have been developing, the different styles or shapes have frequently (but not always) become associated with the place of origin, the name of the designer, or the purposes for which the hook was first made. Comprehensive displays of hooks can be quite daunting. What does the untrained eye look for? Does a fish really know the difference between a long-shanked Kirby and a standard roach hook or, indeed, between a Limerick or a Cincinatti Bass? Of course not. But that doesn't alter the fact that certain differences can and do have an effect on the final result of your efforts to catch a fish, and so it is certainly advisable to keep more than one pattern in your tackle box.

Manufacturers have a curious, but none the less effective method of denoting a hook's size. It is generally accepted that freshwater hooks start at size 1 and get steadily smaller as they progress to sizes 2, 3 and 4. From then on the odd numbers are usually dropped and the sizes go from 6 to 8, 10, 12 and so on until the very small and highly specialist sizes of 22 and 24. The average angler will seldom find it necessary to even consider using anything smaller than a 16 or 18. The very small hooks tend to be the province of the specialist 'match' or 'competition' angler, who might well select a 22 or 24 when baiting with a very slim bodied worm to catch a large number of small fish.

Sea angling hook sizes have the suffix /0. The smallest is 1/0, which gets larger as the range progresses, 2/0, 3/0, 4/0, 5/0 and so on right up to 15/0 and beyond, which are hooks of a size suited to shark weighing hundreds of pounds.

Hooks are secured to the line with a knot suited to either a spade or eyed end.

Freshwater hooks can be either spade end or eyed. Sea hooks are invariably eyed in the conventional manner, but there are specialised hooks which have variations.

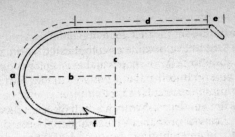

Parts of a hook: a. bend, b. throat, c. gap, d. shank, e. eye, f. point.

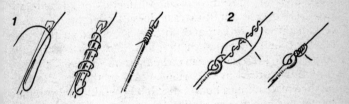

1. How to tie a spade end whipping knot. 2. How to tie on an eyed hook.

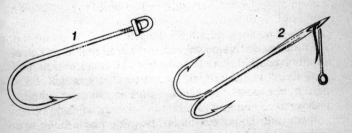

1. Swivelled conger hook. 2. Double bait hook with needle eye.

Hooks are supplied both 'loose' and 'mounted', that is to say factory-tied to a length of monofilament line, which is also loop knotted to afford easy attachment to the main line. I prefer to buy my hooks 'loose' as this is cheaper, and if the hook knot or whipping fails I only have myself to blame. Another important fact is that an additional join is dispensed with if, where possible, the hook is tied direct to the reel line. A joint, however good, is still an additional hazard.

Hooks come in a number of shank lengths, and some are barbed. Points are various, ranging from beak to barbless and on to triangulated.

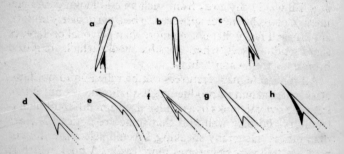

Hook points: a. kirbed, b. straight, c. reversed, d. hollow, e. curved in, f. superior, g. Dublin, h. knife edge.

There are double hooks and trebles, as well as those coloured black, gold, bronze and silver. The choice seems endless. To get to the heart of the matter I suggest that, for all practical purposes, the average freshwater angler would be well served by using crystal bend hooks when fishing maggot and chrysalis baits, and a standard round bend hook when using bread, worm and most other popular coarse angling baits.

Sea anglers will find that a selection of the following should cover most eventualities: fine-wire long-shank eyed hooks will perform well when fishing for flatfish (such as plaice, flounder, dabs); a range of barbed shank, a few beak or in-curve hooks for the middle range such as whiting and bream; and for species such as conger, tope and even large cod, 'Seamaster' hooks with triangulated points can prove extremely effective.

More detailed advice about hook sizes is given in chapter 5, but always remember that using hooks which are either over or undersize is a very common mistake. Always aim at using a hook which matches the bait. A large bait on a small hook, for example, would probably mask the hook tip, and the fish would be lost. A small bait on a large hook would be ignored as a fish would shy away from such an odd looking arrangement. Colour has never appeared to be a particularly important factor. I fancy that it is no more than personal preference that I tend to select, where possible, hooks which are gilt or bronze for freshwater fishing.

All reputable manufacturers can be relied on to use first-class material and to produce high-quality hooks but if you examine several hooks of a similar size from different manufacturers you may well find that some are noticeably finer than others. Generally speaking I would select the thinner hook, as fine wire penetrates more easily. A hook which is well home will take the strain on the strongest part, the bottom of the bend, so there is a greater chance of success. A hook which is only holding on the point and barb will probably straighten or snap. Either way you lose the fish.

When sea fishing for the larger species such as conger, tope, spurdog and bull huss, it is worth considering the penetrating power of a hook with cutting edges on the point. A hook of this type will cut its way through the tough jaw tissue, whereas a hook with the more usual cone-shaped point meets ever-increasing resistance as it goes in. Cost is, of course, an important factor and the simplest hooks are the cheapest.

Floats

Coarse anglers frequently own more floats than they need, and sea anglers rarely have enough. Both have one thing in common – they often use them incorrectly. Basically, a float is required to perform two fundamental tasks: to give visual indication that a fish has taken the bait, and to provide the amount of buoyancy necessary to suspend the bait at a pre-determined depth. Although this may seem relatively sim-

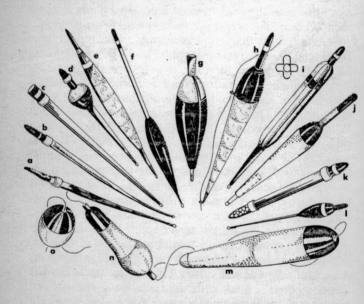

Selection of floats for both freshwater and sea: a. porcupine quill, b. feather quill, c. stick, d. grayling, e. cork Avon, f. antenna, g. bung (pike), h. slider, i. fluted trotter, j. zoomer (metal insert), k. self-cocking (shot loaded), l. bob float, m,n,o. sea floats.

ple, the truth is that float fishing is, at its most complicated, one of the most difficult of all the angling arts.

Probably the most common mistake is the use of a float which is too large. Close behind is the fault of using the wrong type for a particular purpose. Using a float which is oversized means that it sits too high in the water and therefore, as a fish bites at the bait, the float's resistance frightens it.

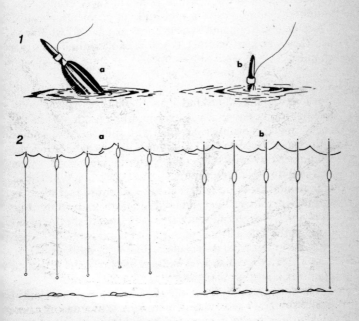

1. a. Oversize float incorrectly shotted causes great resistance which frightens fish. b. Correctly set float causes minimal resistance. 2.a. A bung-type float causes a 'dancing bait'. b. The antenna float will overcome this problem.

To overcome the 'dancing bait' problem caused by the wave action on the 'bung' type float, switch to an antenna style. Correctly set, this type of float will keep the bait steady. Colour is also important – not so much from the fish's point of view as the angler's. Colour vision against a water background can be extremely variable and, strangely, a black-tipped float is sometimes more easily seen than any other colour on a dull day. Find out which colour you can spot against a mixed background – but remember your float might well be 40 or 50 yards away. It also pays to carry a selection of coloured plastic float tips so that a quick change can be made to counter altered conditions.

Float fishing in water which is considerably deeper than your rod is long creates a multitude of problems, most of which can be overcome by using a sliding float. Just how to fish these, and many other types, is explained later in this chapter.

Leads

Without weights of one kind or another it is virtually impossible to arrange either coarse or sea angling tackle. While the coarse angler is mainly concerned with split shot and a range of specialised legering and spinning leads up to about 1oz, the sea angler's weights are generally considerably greater than this – up to a pound or more.

Split shot are small pellets of soft lead cut so that they can be pressed onto the line, and taken off again easily. Only buy shot which is deep and well cut as poor quality shot can both damage the line and fail to open and close correctly. They progress in size from the smallest, dust shot, through sizes 6, 5, 4, 3, 2, 1, BB, AA and AAA to shot approximately $\frac{1}{4}$ inch in diameter known as SSG.

The correct use of shot is one of the basic keys to successful float fishing, so it is essential to carry a reasonably comprehensive supply. A multi-size easy dispenser pack is ideal for this purpose. Plummets are used to check the depth so that the float can be set at the required point on the line. The clip-on-model is spring-loaded and fits cupped around the hook while in use.

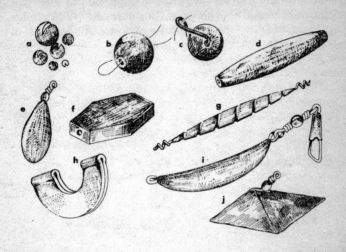

Leads: a. split shot, b. drilled bullet, c. Hillman, d. pierced barrel, e. Arlesy bomb, f. coffin, g. Jardine spiral, h. foldover, i. Wye, j. Capta.

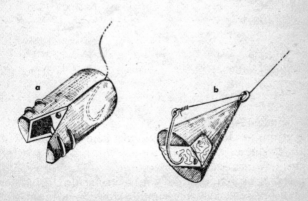

Plummets: a. clip-on, b. cork-insert.

43

Similar remarks apply equally to leger weights and varying water conditions must be met by using various sizes and shapes of lead. Although sea angling normally calls for much heavier weights, the basic principles are similar and an equally comprehensive range is necessary.

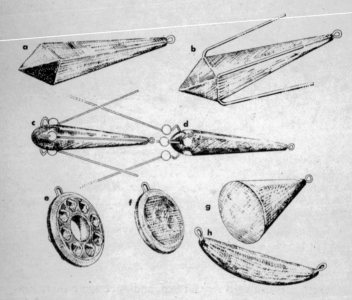

Sea leads: a. pyramid, b. grapnel, c. break-out, d. wires in 'break-out' position, e. grip, f. watch, g. cone, h. spinning or trolling anti-kink.

Miscellaneous
Under this heading are a collection of items used by coarse, sea and game anglers, as well as those which are the province of just one interest.

Landing nets range from the short-handled collapsible trout fisher's net, complete with slip-over clip, to the massive net with telescopic pole used by some specialist carp fishers.

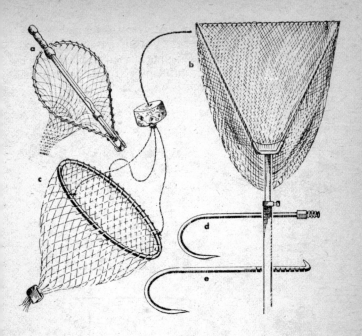

a. Trout net, b. carp net with telescopic handle, c. drop net for pier or sea-wall fishing, d. screw-in gaff, e. whip-on gaff.

Gaffs are also used to land fish, and once again there is a wide selection ranging from expensive telescopic items made from stainless steel to the effective home-made one consisting of a stout pole and gaff hook which is held in position by strong whipping. When not in use, cap the point with a cork.

Coarse fishing keep nets must be large. There is nothing more damaging to a fish than to be held in overcrowded conditions in a small-capacity net.

Many fisheries are covered by strict rules which lay down the minimum measurements and types of nets which can be used by anglers on that water. Never use a net less than 4ft long and 15in in diameter. Bank sticks are used to hold the net in position.

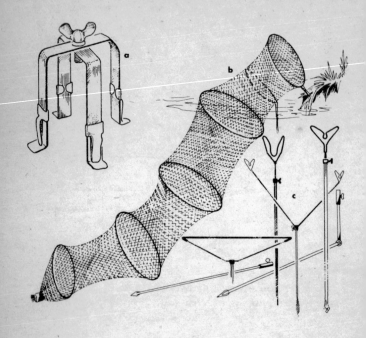

a. Bait spider, b. keep-net, c. selection of bank sticks and rod rests.

Buckles, swivels and booms. These various items are used to assemble the many different styles of terminal tackle. They are often rather expensive and, while on some occasions the use of buckles and swivels cannot be avoided, the angler might find it profitable to dispense with them whenever possible.

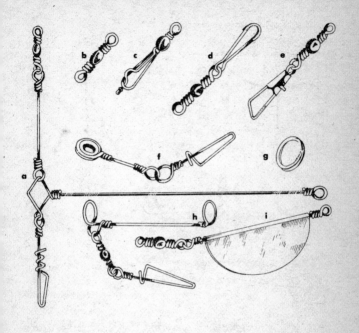

a. Paternoster spreader, b. barrel swivel, c. barrel buckle swivel, d. link spring barrel swivel, e. American snap, f. Kilmore boom, g. split ring, h. Clements boom, i. anti-kink vane.

When arranging spinning tackle, swivels cannot be left out. Although ball-bearing swivels are the most expensive, they are also the most efficient.

Rests, bait boxes and disgorgers. Rod-rests are important to both coarse and sea anglers and there are specialised designs for each.

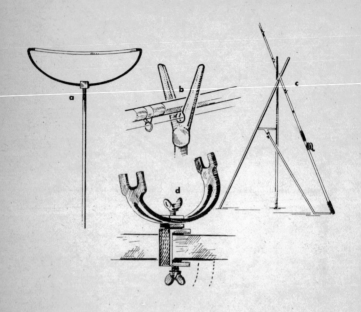

a. Rod rest for float fishing, b. legering, c. beach fishing, d. boat fishing.

The majority of coarse anglers use standard plastic bait containers for maggots, worm and chrysalis. Sea anglers, however, might find a suitably sized wooden box a considerably more useful store, particularly if it is lined with pitch. More information on this subject is given in Chapter 3. Many anglers use surgical-type forceps to remove hooks, particularly where larger, tougher-jawed species are concerned. The smaller Sheffield style or the orthodox V-shape disgorgers are more commonly used when dealing with the smaller species of coarse fish. Carry one on a length of cord looped through a buttonhole or on a lanyard around your neck.

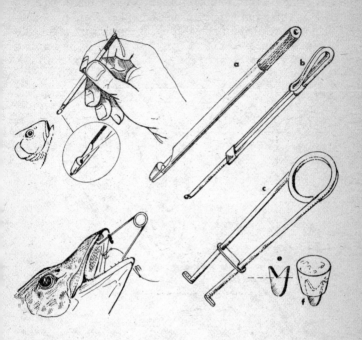

*Disgorgers. a. and b. shown in use. c. Pike gag, shown in use.
d. cut off the points or, e. mask with cork to prevent injury to the
fish.*

Never attempt to remove a hook from a pike's mouth
without first pegging it open with a gag. Always carry two,
one large and the other small, so that fish of various sizes can
be dealt with. To avoid damage to the fish either cover the
points with a cork or flatten them.

Lures and specialised pike fishing tackle. In recent years both
sea and freshwater anglers have, in increasing numbers,
turned to fishing various artificial lures, as well as using dead
fish mounted on specialised hook arrangements.

A dead fish for example, roach, dace or a marine species such as sprat and herring fished on either Avon or Archer tackle can be used for pike fishing, as can any one of literally dozens of plugs.

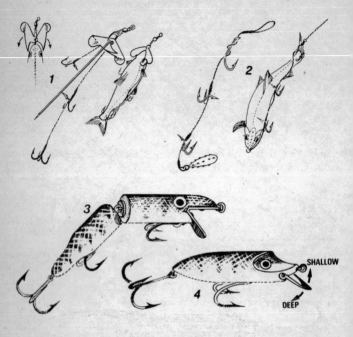

1. Avon snap trolling tackle. 2. Archer tackle. 3. Jointed plug. 4. One piece plug with vane setting.

Trolling tackle is designed to make the bait flutter and twist as it sinks to the bottom after being cast. The bait is then reeled in a short distance and allowed to sink yet again. This action is repeated, with pauses between each 'lift and sink'. Archer tackle enables the angler to use dead fish instead of an orthodox metal or plastic spinner.

1. *Voblex spinner. The soft rubber head is a cleverly disguised anti-kink weight. 2. Ondex blade spinner. 3. Colorado spoon.*

Sea angling lures includes pirks as well as a variety of bars and imitation eels.

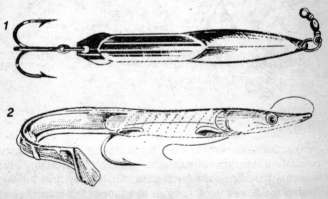

1. *Pirk. 2. Redgill artificial sand eel.*

Knives and scissors. Most anglers carry a knife of one sort or another, and for sea fishermen a really stout blade with a sharp point is an essential for not only cutting bait but also killing some species. A pair of scissors is also a vital accessory, and is much easier to use than a knife when cutting short ends of nylon after tying a knot. Another tool of great use is the weed cutter which is equipped with a screw thread and fits into a bank stick or landing-net handle. A punch complete with a range of heads to provide bread baits of varying size and a bread cube press are two small yet incredibly useful items.

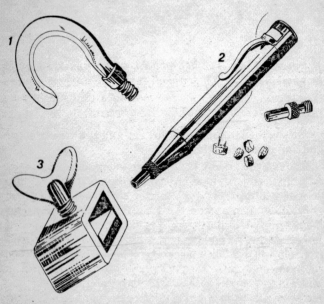

1. Weed cutter. 2. Bread punch. 3. Bread cube press.

There are many other pieces of equipment, both small and large, all of which form part of the angler's equipment. For example there are specialised items for placing groundbait close to the baited hook, as well as a range of containers for hooks, floats and a variety of smaller items.

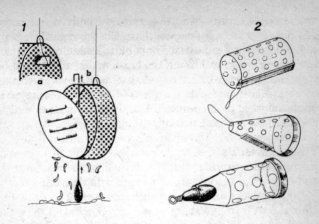

1. Bait dropper. a. The dropper is attached to the line by passing the hook through the loop and inserting the hook into cork. b. When the weighted bar catch touches the bottom, the hinged lid is released, depositing the feed. 2. Swimfeeders.

Rod holdalls, umbrellas, even one-man tents and a selection of chairs and stools are part of the paraphenalia, but a selection such as this would not be complete without reference to clothing and personal aids to comfortable fishing. Wellingtons or waders are essential, and make sure they are not a tight fit. When buying leave room for both air circulation and thick woollen stockings. There are few conditions more uncomfortable than cold feet. Warm undergarments and windproof outer are needed with waterproofs that protect your neck, and also cover the top of your boots. A steady drip from a short plastic coverall will rapidly soak your trousers and socks.

Sea anglers can do a lot worse than buying a professional fisherman's long waterproof smock. These are really excellent for both beach and boat fishing. Polaroid glasses are invaluable as reflected glare can prove almost intolerable. These glasses also aid vision down into water, a fact which can be most helpful when, for example, bringing a fish to the net. The type which float and have flip-up lenses are most useful. It is estimated that it's possible to lose at least a fifth of one's body warmth through the head, and it might even be more if one is a bit thin on top. As well as being an extremely useful pin-cushion for flies, a deer-stalker or helmet-style hat offers valuable protection to the back of the neck as well as checking the escaping warmth.

Fly-fishing tackle
Fly rods are designed to throw or cast a line, whereas most sea and coarse fishing rods are concerned with delivering terminal tackle which in itself has sufficient weight to draw line from the reel. In fly fishing we are concerned with the art of presenting an imitation fly or insect which, for all practical casting purposes, is weightless. The weight which is necessary for casting is therefore built into the line. It is important to realise that there is a very special relationship between fly rod and line, one which is completely different to that between, for example, a beach casting rod and the monofilament used to cast a 6 or 8oz lead.

Having established that it is the line which provides the weight necessary to get the bait (fly) to the fish, it is now essential to appreciate that these lines are constructed in a variety of ways, and each has its own special code or marking. Some lines are made to sink, which allows the fly to be presented on the bottom, while others float on the surface. There is also a specialised line which is constructed in such a way that just the last section – possibly some 3 to 5 yards – will sink, while the remainder floats. Today, within the Air Cel and Wet Cel ranges there are lines which will float for ever without further treatment, and sinking lines which go down at no less than four different speeds. Within these three groups there are lines of differing weights, the most popular lighter lines being 4 and 5, getting heavier as the numbers progress.

There are also various 'types' of line, and by this I mean ones which have a diameter that changes in a pre-determined way because of their special built-in characteristics. A double taper line has a centre section which has a uniform thickness, tapering to a smaller diameter at each end. They have the advantage of being what might be described as two lines in one. When one end wears, the line can be reversed. The 'weight forward' line is designed for longer casting, but unlike the double taper (DT) it cannot be reversed.

Normally, both DT and WF lines are 30 yards long, but a 'shooting taper' (ST) is only 30ft. Where, for example, the angler is faced with a large expanse of water and it is obvious that, for a variety of reasons, the fish are some distance off, his problem is getting the fly out a greater distance than a DT or WF line would achieve. The ST is, in essence, no more than the belly and front taper of a WF line. However, when attached to a nylon monofilament line, the ST provides sufficient weight to pull or draw an amount of monoline behind it – and the required extra distance is reached.

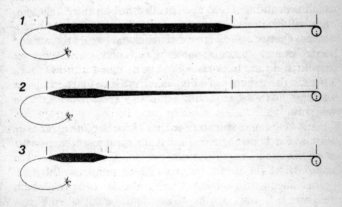

1. Double taper. 2. Weight forward. 3. Shooting taper.

It must be appreciated that these diagrams are merely representations of the various lines and that each weight has its own special dimensions. Anglers must know what the various codes mean, because the Association of Fishing Tackle Manufacturers (AFTM) use these symbols to identify the different lines and, in turn, to relate them to specific rods. For example: F – floating line; S – sinking line; F/S – floating sinking line; DT – double taper; WF – weight forward; ST – shooting taper. Remember also the weight classification: 4, 5, 6 and so on. The various symbols result in a fly line being coded as, for example, AFTM DT8S or AFTM WF7F. In other words, the Association of Fishing Tackle Manufacturers classify the line as being a double taper 8 weight sinking line, or a weight forward 7 weight floating line.

Fly rods are not manufactured to such strict standards for a variety of obscure reasons. Every fly rod from a reputable manufacturer is specifically designed to be matched with a particular weight of line, and unless the rod and line are suited, casting efficiency will suffer. The importance of the relationship between rod and line cannot be overstated. For example, for fishing moorland streams or brooks, where small flies and fine leaders are called for, an extremely light rod could be matched with a DT4 or a WF4. As circumstances change – and here we are back once again to 'fish and environment' – so more powerful rods and heavier lines are required. A light trout rod would be matched with a DT6 for example, a medium rod would need an 8 line, and perhaps a 9 or 10 would be used in conjunction with a powerful salmon or sea trout rod.

It is also important to note that there is quite a range of specialised fly fishing reels, and using the one which matches both rod and line is essential for successful angling. For example, a 2¾in diameter reel would be completely filled if it were loaded with a DT4 line. Remember also that your line is just 30 yards long, half of which might be out when a large fish is hooked. The remaining 15 yards could be totally inadequate to play the fish, and the resulting fiasco might well loose you a specimen fish. So make sure that the reel is suited to both the rod and line, as well as to the conditions.

I would never have less than 25 yards of backing, even fishing a very small stream, and I always feel happier with at least 50 yards. Where there is a good chance that a really large fish may take, then 100 yards or more of backing can be more than useful.

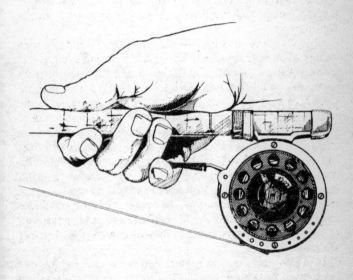

A reel with an automatic rewind, such as the Mitchell 710, offers a capacity to store 80 yd of 20lb BS backing as well as a 6 line.

The rewind trigger is controlled by the little finger, and such a reel solves the problem of getting loose line onto the spool rapidly.

When using an ST line, additional consideration must be given to the amount of line which the angler can cast. The important point is to remember that these facts have a vital effect on angling efficiency, and therefore both choose and assemble tackle with care to get the best out of what is available.

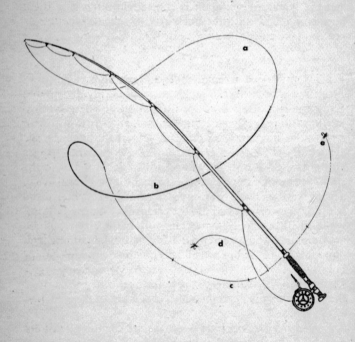

Assembled fly fishing outfit: a. backing, b. fly line (reduced in length for clarity), c. tapered cast, d. dropper, e. point fly.

The cast, or leader, is a length of nylon running from the tip of the fly line. For the best results it should be 'tapered', starting, for example, with 3ft of 9lb BS nylon, joined to 2½ft of 6lb and finally 2ft 3lb BS. There is no set formula, the amount of leader depends upon the length of rod, and the various strengths of nylon used are related to the weight of line. Experience is the key, but most anglers are best served by buying a manufactured leader. Once again it must be realised that here is yet another vital link between angler and fish. The reel, rod and line can all be in balance, but an incorrect leader will mean the fly will not land as it should, and the whole presentation is ruined. So often it is these finer points which, in the final analysis, decide whether or not you take a fish.

Freshwater tackle arrangements and methods

Fish, like animals in the jungle, are not evenly distributed across the lake, river or sea bed. Many are shoaling species, moving from area to area for environmental reasons, or in response to migratory instincts brought about either by the availability of food or the urge to reproduce. Other species are solitary creatures, only joining their fellows during the spawning season. For the rest of the year they may well live in a fairly well defined area, feeding on smaller fish which come within range. Some feed almost exclusively on the bottom, while others take food at midwater or from the surface. There are those fish which prefer a moving bait, while others look more favourably at one which lays quietly on the bottom or bobs seductively on the surface. Fish may also change their feeding habits at various times of the year but, fortunately, they are never totally predictable. That is one of the great joys of the sport.

Leger tackle. In an effort to outwit the changing attitudes adopted by his quarry, the angler has developed an enormous number and variations of tackle arrangements.

A simple rig which can be used in a stream to present a bait which moves along with the current. To prevent it rolling, change the lead and use one designed to hold, such as Coffin

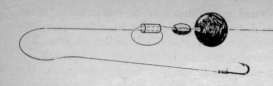

Leger: hook tied direct to reel line. Valve rubber stop bead and drilled bullet.

and Capta. Other stops which can be used to prevent the weight sliding down to the hook include:

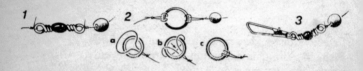

1. Swivel. 2. Split ring and method of fixing. 3. American snap.

In canals or very slow flowing rivers, a link leger arrangement can be useful as it creates a minimal disturbance when it hits the water. A large splash made by a bigger weight could disturb a shoal of feeding fish.

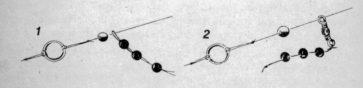

Link legers. 1. Trace, split ring, bead on reel line and shot on nylon loop. 2. Trace, ring, bead and barrel swivel holding nylon and split shot.

The number and size of shot used depends entirely upon factors such as distance to be cast, current and depth, but never use more than is necessary to operate successfully. Swim feeders are also excellent for this style of angling. They act both as a weight and as a vehicle to take a fish attracting feed to within a foot or so of the hook.

Swim feeder: a leger hook tied direct to the reel line; a split ring looped into the line; a bead and then a swivel carry the nylon trace holding the swim feeder.

One extremely simple rig can be used for both 'upstream legering' as well as 'free lining'.

Hook tied direct to the reel line, with two split shot on the line just above the hook.

A variety of bite-detecting devices have been developed, ranging from electric alarms to pieces of silver paper on the line.

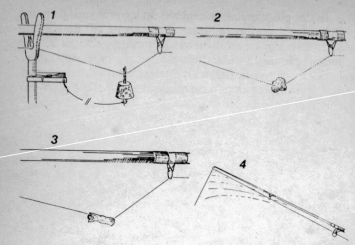

1. Grip and peg indicator. 2. Dough-bob. 3. Silver foil.
4. Quiver tip.

These simple methods are capable of infinite variation according to both weather conditions and bank situations. For example, a very strong wind buffeting the rod tip can register false bites. This might be overcome by rearranging both rod and indicator.

The sunken line runs to the rod tip under water; a peg is clamped on a bucket handle with a cork and grip lying in the bottom of the bucket.

In this position the line and rod tip are protected from the breeze, and the bite indicator is also sheltered. Both swing and quiver tips are excellent bite indicators, although I prefer the latter as they are less affected by strong wind. A swing tip is more effective if used with a target board. A selection of both quiver and swing tips are necessary to match the various conditions which occur.

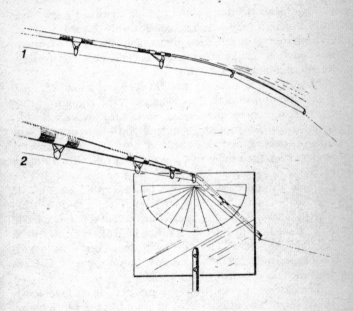

1. Quiver tip. 2. Swing tip and target board.

Carp fishing, an occupation which frequently consists of many hours of patient waiting, is often a night-time exercise. To avoid missing fish, and also to remove the necessity of concentrating hour after hour on a piece of silver paper, many carp fishers use electric bite alarms. They can give both a sound and light warning. When fishing a moving bait – for example one being rolled over a gravel bed or drawn back downstream – the only really efficient bite indicator is the angler's sense of touch. The vibrations which travel along the line need a lot of translation, but this is an art which is only learned slowly. However, even a complete novice will not fail to realise what is happening if and when a barbel or chub bites hard on a bait fished on a rolling leger. In angling, some lessons are soon learned!

Float tackle. In this style of angling there are a few basic rules which, if followed, help considerably towards success. Accept that you will need more than one float – various methods and changing conditions can only be met effectively by altering tackle and tactics.

Never use a float larger than is necessary, and always pay great attention to both the placing and the amount of shot used between hook and float. It saves time, as well as additional disturbance of the water, if you know exactly how much shot is needed to 'cock' each float in your box. Some anglers keep their floats in a special 'float roll' with a slot for each one. The sections are marked – 4 No. 3, or 2 BB, for example – so the angler can pick whatever shot is required.

A float which is too large for the job it has to do sits too high in the water and an excessive amount of shot is needed to make it settle. A float which is riding high offers far too much resistance to a fish, a fact which will almost certainly make it reject the bait. Carefully arranged shot of the right size can alter the way a float reacts to a 'bite'.

The diagram shows two very simple tackle arrangements. In (1) the fish would draw the float under, but by changing the shot and setting the float so that the tip is just at the surface, (2) the whole method is altered. A bottom feeding fish such as a tench or bream has only to mouth the bait and the float lifts. That is the time to strike.

When arranging shot for the 'lift' method (2) it is essential to match both shot and float so that the lead is only just enough to overcome the float's buoyancy. Too much lead and the fish will reject the bait as the shot must be fixed close by – no more than 60 mm from the hook.

Another factor which has a great bearing on the success or

otherwise of float fishing is line control. Avoid a loop of line between rod tip and float. This will impede the strike and any delay results in lost fish. A strong breeze can cause the line to bow, with the result that both float and tackle are drawn away from the target area. Yet another change in tactics will overcome this problem.

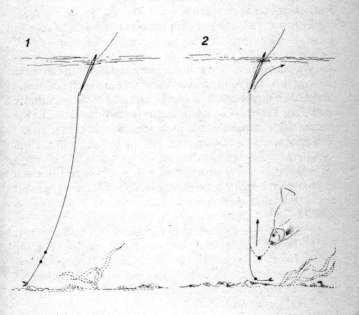

1. Quill float with two shot close to the hook with bait just tripping the bottom. Line fixed top and bottom. 2. Same quill float with one large shot set for the 'lift' method. Float tip just at surface. Line fixed top and bottom.

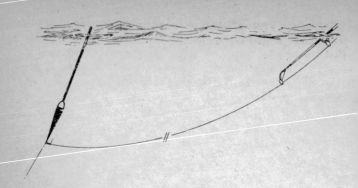

Ruffled surface: the antenna float is well down, the line is fixed to the bottom of the float and sunk to rod tip which is also under water.

To achieve this effect and also place the tackle in the target area, cast just beyond the mark and reel in slowly. This will draw the baited hook back to the target as the line is drawn under the surface. Laying-on is a very traditional method. A taking fish is usually signalled by the float 'dithering' before either lying flat or sliding under.

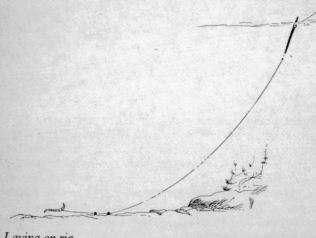

Laying-on rig.

Restricted areas of clear water between reed beds or lily pads be fished very efficiently with either paternoster or float leger rig.

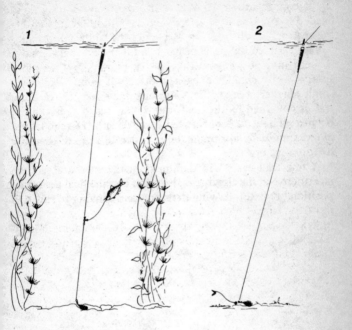

1. Paternoster. 2. Float leger.

In these cases the amount of lead has no bearing on the float as the weight is acting as an anchor. Therefore when using a float leger, employ the smallest, most slim-bodied float that works efficiently, as there will be only minimal resistance as the fish takes the bait. There is, however, a slightly different situation when operating a paternoster rig. If, for example, a small live-bait were being used to attract perch, then the balance must be struck between the 'weight' of the bait and the float's buoyancy.

One of the most difficult of all the float fishing methods is the hightly efficient 'on the drop' style. Fishing 'on the drop' is, as the term implies; a method in which the fish can be caught literally as the bait drops or sinks through the water. Great concentration as well as a large amount of skill is needed to use this style effectively, as both immaculate timing and tackle control is the essence of the whole operation.

The float could be a peacock quill with a balsa body, secured into position by two shot at point 'A'. Two more shot, slightly smaller ones, are placed at point 'B', and a single smaller shot at 'C'. Naturally, the exact size of these shot is governed by the float, but remember to keep it all in balance. The length of line between 'A' and 'D' (the baited hook) should be approximately 25 per cent more than the depth of water.

A few trial casts will demonstrate the measurable time lapse between the rig hitting the water and the float assuming position (1) (see following diagram) and moving to position

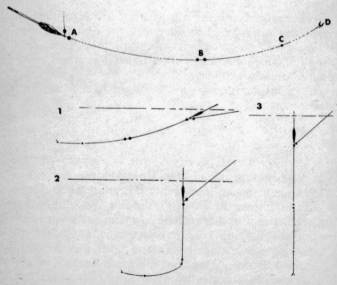

Three stages of 'on the drop'.

(2) under the influence of the second pair of shot. The single and lightest shot then swings into line and the float settles into its final position, (3).

As the bait is sinking a fish might well intercept it, and this action would break the sequence of events, namely: float at $\frac{1}{4}$ cock, pause, $\frac{1}{2}$ cock, pause, fully settled. The slightest deviation from that order and timing should be countered with a strike. This is a very popular match fishing tactic as it gives the angler a chance to catch both the smaller fish which could be feeding at mid-water or close to the surface, as well as the larger ones, such as bream, which could be on the bottom.

A 'zoomer' float can also be used for fishing 'on the drop' but, as these floats are weighted, the two shots adjacent to the float are not needed. The lightest shot is still at the bottom, but under no circumstances should it ever rest on the bed, if it did, the float would not settle in the 'cocked' position. A 'zoomer' type float gives the additional weight which is often necessary when either trying to cast further, or counter a strong wind.

Remember, when using heavier floats and leads there is extra strain on the line. For example, a near 1lb BS line may be perfectly adequate for casting very light float tackle, but a 3 or 4lb BS line would be far more suited to casting a heavy 'zoomer' plus the extra lead.

The sliding float allows very deep water to be fished with relative ease.

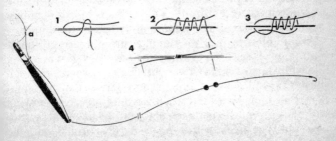

Sliding float: how to tie a stop knot (a).

Both 'stick' and quill floats can be used to fish stretches of running water, a technique called 'trotting the stream'.

Trotting. Cast to point X. Allow the tackle to drift to Y. Pause to allow the bait to lift. This will often result in a bite. The retrieve is to point Z. Repeat the process.

Never let the line get out of control. A great slack bow lying across the stream will not only make striking difficult, it will also pull the float away from its intended course. To check a belly of line, just lift and 'roll' the rod tip in an upstream direction. Done quickly, this should flick the line back into its correct attitude. This action is called 'mending the line', and it is also an important fly fishing technique.

A wind blowing over the run of a current creates difficult conditions. At sea it isn't long before wave tops start breaking into white foam, and in a river, although the waves are much smaller, a similar set of circumstances arise. Bait presentation is all important, and when a strong breeze is blowing with the current there is a tendency for the line to act rather like a sail. The breeze will also catch the float tip and, with the additional surface drift, there is a danger that the baited hook will be totally out of position.

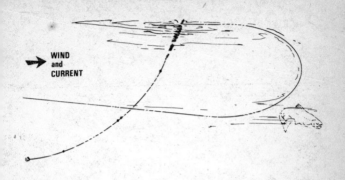

Line and float preceding the baited hook with the bait trailing behind at mid-water.

This situation can be countered by fixing the line only to the bottom of the float. If additional line drag is needed to slow the float down even more, sink several yards of line running back from the float. Wipe the section of line through a pad moistened with detergent which will help to make it sink.

Casting into the wind also creates problems, but carefully considered shot grouping can be an answer. Concentrate the bulk of the weight closer to the hook and use a heavier float. Deep and fast-flowing water is also difficult to float fish. Light tackle may well be swept out of the reach of your control before the bait has settled. These conditions might be countered by using a heavier float such as a 'ducker' or an Avon, and adjusting the shot pattern to match. It might also be possible to cast upstream for a distance, so that the tackle has additional time to settle, but always remember to keep your line under control. Never allow a great bow to appear as the float comes back downstream. The drag created

Float tackle with the line sunk and the bait swinging and preceding the float.

by the excess line will not only pull the float away from its intended path, but also an efficient strike will be prevented. Never allow the float to pass the point at which you lose control – in other words, out of sight – or run on to such a distance that efficient striking is impossible.

Except for the few occasions when circumstances make fishing a sunken line a necessity, it pays to have it on the surface when float fishing. Not only is it easier to keep under control, but trying to pick up a sunken line can completely kill a strike. To help the line float, draw it through a pad impregnated with Mucillin, a special product made to make line float.

Spinning tackle. Line twist is probably the most annoying problem posed by this style of angling. It can only be overcome by using the right tackle but, unfortunately these days, this can be an expensive proposition. Anglers frequently dispense with both swivels and leads, tying the spinner direct to the reel line. This has two effects: the lure is drawn directly towards the rod tip, and the line is twisted to an incredible

Spinning tackle assembly. The fold over lead (a) can be used over the reel line (c) to replace the Wye lead (b).

degree, with the result that after several casts the line becomes totally unmanageable.

This basic assembly can be varied to suit differing conditions. To cast further do not just add more or larger weight as this will only unbalance the rig to such an extent that the lead will dominate during the flight and the spinner hooks will probably tangle with the line. Increase the size and weight of the lure to compensate for a heavier Wye lead or foldover. Deep rivers and strong currents call for the use of heavier tackle, but remember not to overload either rod or line.

The casting action imparts an amount of energy to the lead and spinner, and much of this energy is used to draw line from the spool and through the rod rings. If the line is heavier than it should be, distance will be lost. It is also important to point the rod in the direction taken by the flighting tackle, as the greater the angle between rod and line of flight, the more friction there is at the top ring.

Accurate casting is essential. A succession of wild throws is not only bad angling but it can be enormously expensive. There are few things more annoying than looking at a selection of your own spinners decorating trees and reeds on a bank you cannot reach. Casting accurately is not only essential to minimise tackle losses. The inability to place a lure where required leaves the angler with less places to fish, and a large number of these spots are going to be just the sort of area a pike or large perch could be lurking.

A gusty head or side wind can sometimes be countered by using a small but heavy-bodied spinner, and the hazards associated with fishing around weeds can be reduced by using a lure such as a 'Reflex weedless'.

Plugs can replace spinners, and where the water is heavily weeded, try a floating plug, one which can be made to 'skitter' and splash its way across the surface. It's amazing how sometimes a pike will 'rise' to such a lure.

Sea angling tackle arrangements and methods

Basically, the tackle arrangements used by sea anglers are similar to freshwater rigs. The main differences are strength plus a greater use of corrosion-resistant materials.

Leger. As the diagram shows, the basic plan is identical (ie a weight running freely on the reel line, and prevented from reaching the hook by a 'stop'). Only the scale and detail is changed to suit either fish or environment.

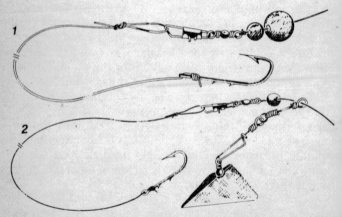

Leger rigs: 1. Beak hook and serrated shank on trace to American snap; bead and pierced bullet. An assembly of this type could be used for bass fishing where the bait could roll over snag-free ground. 2. As in (1) but with Kilmore boom and Capta lead.

The Kilmore boom carries the heavier lead, and the weight is designed to hold the tackle steady in a predetermined position. A lead of this type will hold well in sand but, when lifted, its shape does not offer huge resistance to being reeled in.

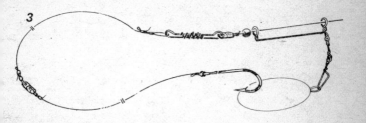

3. Leger tackle for ray or conger: Seamaster hook, Steelon trace (3ft), swivel half way, screw link to swivel, bead, Clements boom.

A hook of this type gives excellent penetration of the creature's tough mouth tissue. The nylon covered steel trace is both flexible and strong. Its flexibility aids bait presentation, and the steel core is designed to prevent the ray's teeth grinding through. While lying in the tide run, the bait may twist, and the hooked fish may also 'spin' while being brought in. The two swivels prevent the main line from being affected. Large fish must be freed from the rod and line as quickly as possible to prevent chaos. A screw link enables this to be done. The Clements boom carries a heavy weight with great efficiency, keeping the trace running away in the desired manner. Various weights can be used, ranging from large Capta to any of the others designed to grip or hold to the sea bed efficiently.

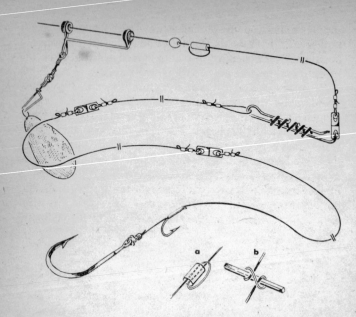

Leger rig for tope: Seamaster hook with one smaller hook whipped onto trace just above to hold large bait in position. 6ft Steelon trace, two heavy-duty box swivels. Screw link to HD swivel to reel line. Clements boom 'stopped' further up reel line with valve rubber stop (a), bead and boom. (Matchstick stop (b) separately.)

When deliberately fishing for tope it is advisable to use an extra long trace for two reasons. One, it enables the fish, which, despite its size, is relatively wary, to pick up and inspect the bait without feeling the resistance of a heavy lead weight and the additional drag of the line running from 'stop' to rod top. And two, tope are very powerful fish with an extremely rough skin. During the course of a battle the line might become wrapped around its body which may well result in an ordinary nylon or braided line fraying and breaking.

As an alternative to a valve rubber stop, a matchstick held in a clove hitch can be used. Some prefer this arrangement as the matchstick can be snapped by drawing it against the rod's top ring. This allows more line to be reeled in, making the length between weight and hook much shorter, and the landing that much easier.

Paternoster. Beach casting techniques are frequently favoured by this arrangement, particularly so if a bomb-shaped lead is used. A weight of this general shape will, when cast, flight with the heaviest section forward, an attitude which goes a long way towards minimising the possibility of the baited hooks and main line becoming tangled. Casting leger tackle with the force necessary to cover 100 yards or more can result in the weight taking the leading position, and the hook(s) and trace twisting around the reel line. A mess of this sort laying on the sea bed is hardly likely to catch any fish.

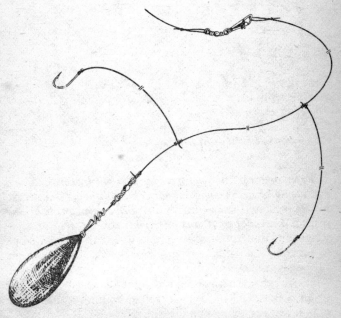

Paternoster rigs: bomb lead; spiral lead link; two hook trace to American snap.

When boat fishing some choose a wire paternoster or similar arrangement.

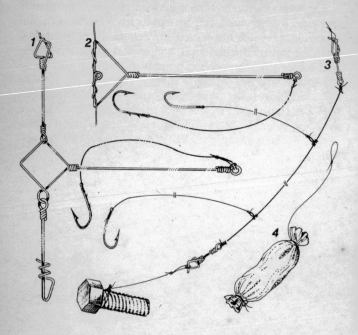

1. *Paternoster rig with wire spreader.* 2. *French boom.*
3. *Paternoster with two hooks; barrel buckle at both weight and reel line end. A short length of nylon is tied around an old bolt as weight.* 4. *Small bag of sand as weight.*

Rough, snag strewn ground, is not the easiest to fish; it can claim a lot of tackle. Using a 'rotten bottom' is one of the easiest ways of combating this situation.

The length of nylon holding the makeshift weight is much weaker than the remainder of the tackle. If the 'weight' becomes fixed, a smart tug will snap the bottom link, thus saving expensive buckles, hooks, line and possibly a valuable amount of fish. A variety of expendable items can be used as weights for a situation such as this. When fishing from a boat, or possibly a pier or jetty, a rig which combines both leger and paternoster styles can be extremely efficient. It is an arrangement which has served me well on many occasions, catching species ranging from conger and ray, to gurnard, cod, whiting and haddock.

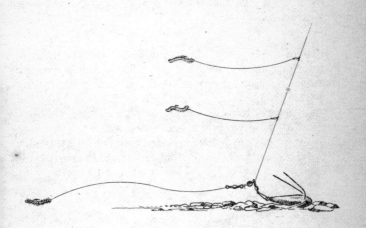

5. *Leger and two flyers.*

Float fishing is also widely practised, and a float and spoon rig is an excellent method for taking flounders. Float tackle must be arranged so that it can be adjusted easily and often as the tide ebbs and flows. Where, for example, a tide produces a 12ft rise and fall, in the first hour the depth changes by 1ft, in the second hour there is an additional 2ft alteration, followed by 3ft in both of the following two hours. During the fifth and sixth hours the change is 2ft and 1ft respectively. In just 30 minutes your bait could be lifted by 1½ft, and so pass right over where the fish are feeding.

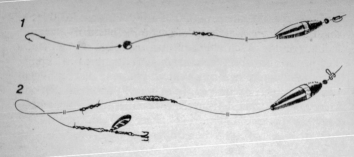

1. Float tackle with valve rubber stop. 2. Float and spoon rig with rubber-band stop.

Although here we are discussing float fishing tactics in a marine environment, the basic principles of float buoyancy, shotting and visual acceptability mentioned earlier in this chapter still apply.

An estuary or harbour will often provide ideal conditions for working a baited spoon. This is basically a technique for flounder fishing which was developed mainly by the late John P. Garrard – and his book *Sea Angling with the Baited Spoon* is a fascinating study of the subject.

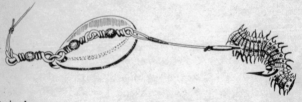

Baited spoon.

Although it is a simple rig, and the method very straightforward, it can be difficult for a newcomer to this style of angling to get both balance and rhythm operating together. A baited spoon is fished with the tide, but to work successfully it must be trailed slightly faster. Secure the rod with a lanyard, and also the oars so that a sudden grab for the rod doesn't leave you watching helplessly as they drift away.

The tackle, baited with king rag, is trailed astern, and a steady pull should set the craft moving at a rate just slightly faster than the current. A rhythmical pulse of the rod tip will reflect the twisting beat of the spoon. Rowing too fast will bring the tackle away from the fish which tend to move and feed with the tide run.

A 'driftline' fished in the tide run as it flows over a sand or shingle bar, around a jetty or pier supports, is an interesting and simple way of catching really large fish, especially bass. At least three-quarters of the bass over 6lb that I have caught have been taken on a drift line, and mainly on sand eel bait. The young of many species are unable to swim against the tide, and are therefore swept along with it. A shoal of such small creatures caught up in a strong current running over a sand bar or reef would be congregated into a tight mass of food. It is here that bass can be found taking advantage of nature's bounty.

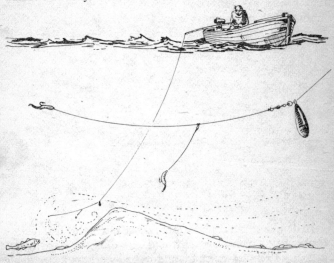

Boat angler fishing a sand bar with detail of a simple tackle arrangement.

Boat anglers drift fishing for species such as bass, plaice and flounders can use Wander tackle, an arrangement which at one time was even used by some professional fishermen. They, of course, used a dozen or more lines from one small craft, continually working the lines in sequence.

The basic tackle arrangements described so far are capable of being varied in many different ways to suit both individual and local fishing conditions. For example, a small white plastic spoon can be added to a three-hook trace when flounder fishing.

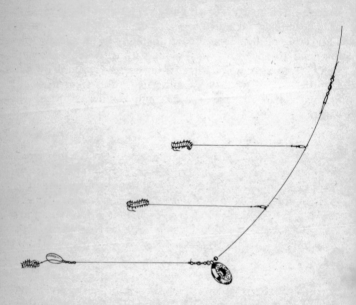

Three-hook trace with spoon.

In deep water and where there is a chance of big fish such as conger of 60lb and over, I would be looking at trace line of perhaps 100lb BS or more, and forged steel hooks, perhaps size 10/0 or even larger. In other words, tackle and techniques to match both fish and environment.

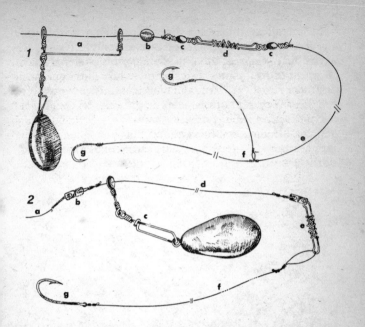

1. a. Clements boom and lead running on 40lb BS main line.
b. Bead. c. Swivels. d. Screw link. e. 4ft 50lb trace. f. Blood
loop. g. 6/0 or 8/0 Seamaster hooks to suit fish being caught.
2. a. Wire line to heavy duty swivel. b. Secured with a Haywire
twist. c. Kilmore boom running on d. 6ft 80lb BS nylon covered
wire. e. Screw link. f. 12 inch 80lb BS nylon covered steel wire
hook trace. g. 10/0 Seamaster hook.

And this is particularly true when hunting for really big
fish in deep water where fierce tidal currents and other
natural hazards combine to create the most difficult and
demanding conditions the sea angler is ever likely to
encounter.

Wrecks lying in several hundred feet of water, and inhabited by huge ling, pollack, conger and other species pose a
whole range of problems which, under more usual conditions, the sea angler never encounters. For example, 300ft of

heavy line offers quite extraordinary resistance to a strong tidal flow, which forces the angler to use a really heavy lead to get the baited hook down to the fish. At this point we enter the world of rod harness, groin protectors, rods equipped with roller rings, very large and powerful reels and probably wire line. At current prices, just the rod and reel could cost well in excess of £200.

Wreck fishing is a specialised form of sea angling, and to take part the angler needs to either charter, or be a member of a party on board, a professional boat organised for this sport.

Wreck fishing equipment. 1. Angler in full harness using heavy duty rod and reel. 2. Groin protector. 3. Roller rings and end ring, essential with wire line. 4. Method of attaching the Mustad Seamaster hook. 5. Double crimps to form loop. 6. Single crimp with heavy duty split ring. 7. Heavy duty swivel.

Fly fishing tackle arrangements and methods

There are two basic fly fishing styles – wet and dry. One is the art of presenting a fly or imitation insect under the water, the other is concerned with fishing on the surface. Wet flies are frequently fished in a team of three, but this is not a standard, as sometimes only one is used.

There is a vast array of flies, many of which are totally unlike any natural insect, being little more than fish-attracting lures. As such, when cast and then recovered quite rapidly, they lure in much the same way as a spinner will do.

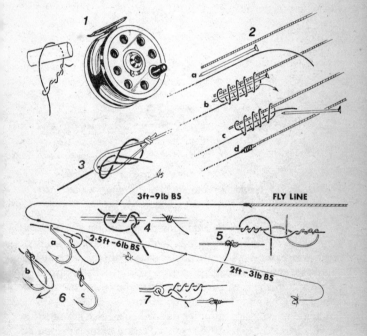

1. Fly reel and knot for securing backing to reel. 2. Needle knot to fix both backing and leader to fly line. 3. Figure of eight knot for tying leader to fly line. 4. and 5. Cast for fishing three wet flies, showing knots in detail. Also note BS of leader sections. 6. Turle knot. 7. A tucked half blood knot attaching flies to leader.

This style of wet fly fishing, while undoubtedly successful, soon degenerates into an automatic sequence which, as an excercise in angling technique, has little to commend it. A far more interesting method is to use flies which imitate natural creatures, and fish them in such a way that trout take them for what they are intended to be.

A team of three flies can be made to imitate insects moving towards the surface where they would take wing. When a strong breeze is ruffling the surface, trout will often be fooled into rising to the 'bob' or second dropper if it is worked across the wave tops. The bob fly can appear to be an insect struggling to get airborne.

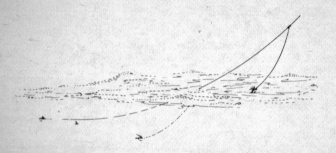

Bob fly on the surface with tail and first dropper underwater.

Nymph fishing is a development of wet fly fishing, the artificial nymphs being skilfully tied imitations of a variety of natural creatures. The theory is very simple. The angler offers an imitation of the trout's food, such as pupae or nymphs, which, in due time, rise from the bed to the surface where they hatch into a winged creature.

On a hot, windless summer day, when all else has failed to move a fish, I have tempted trout to take a nymph presented right on the bottom. The artificial creature was given plenty of time to settle, and was only recovered in a series of very occasional 'twitches'. Nymph fishing is an art all on its own, and one which is not easily learned, but probably the greatest single mistake made by anglers using this method is being in

A selection of nymphs and bugs: a. Chomper. b. Buzzer pupa.
c. Corixa. d. Olive nymph. e. Polystickle. f. Butcher. g. Worm
fly. h. Zulu.

a hurry. Natural creatures do not move around rapidly, and
therefore an imitation which does will probably be ignored.

Briefly, the nymph angler must develop a very stealthy
approach, taking advantage of whatever cover there is, and
use a pattern which resembles the natural food in the water
being fished. Only wade when absolutely necessary, and even
then do it very carefully. Once a fish has been disturbed it will
be some time before it settles, so tread softly, and move
slowly.

Keep the tackle simple, a light to medium rod, perhaps,
with matching DT floating line and a tapered nylon leader
about 12ft long. Smear Mucillin onto that part of the leader
which is not required to sink. If there is a congregation of
pupae just below the surface, then no more than about a foot
of leader should be allowed to sink. If the nymph is to be
fished on the bottom, then act according to depth. When
fishing in deep water use a nymph made for such conditions.
It will have some copper or lead wire under the dressing.

A 'take' is signalled by the line moving at the point it enters
the water. Any suspicious movement warrants a response
from the angler who, if he waits until the fish is felt, will miss
far more than he ever catches. A nymph can also be cast to an
individual fish – in much the same way as one would offer a
dry fly. In fact, the steady development of nymph fishing has
opened a whole new field of both exciting and highly rewarding angling endeavour.

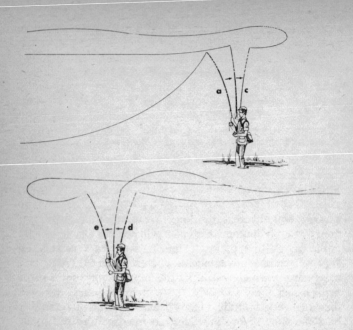

Lift the rod smartly through (a) to the position (c). The line now loops backwards until it reaches the position shown in (d). The pull of the extended line is the signal to force the rod forward to (e). Lowering the rod until it is horizontal will allow the impetus of the line to extend forward and down to the water.

Although the casting action for both wet and dry fly fishing is similar, terminal tackle for the latter is usually a single fly on a tapered cast, rather than the two or three associated with wet fly fishing. The flies themselves are frequently excellent imitations of natural creatures found on the water. It is often the case that fish in a particular stream or lake will only rise to a limited number of flies, and sometimes only one pattern will catch fish. The secret is to know which fly and when. This is knowledge only experience and help from others can provide.

Like nymph fishing, dry fly fishing calls for a gentle approach, sympathy with your surroundings, an understanding of the way your quarry is likely to act, and the ability to be able to cast fairly accurately and gently. Many dry fly anglers prefer to cast only to a rising fish and on some waters this is the accepted way. Dropping a fly onto a stretch of water thought to hold a fish will often tempt one to rise, and indeed a fast stream with a very broken surface calls for this general approach as it is almost impossible to spot a rise. Once a rise is spotted, get within casting distance as quietly as possible. Learn to move cautiously while holding your rod, butt forward, and at an angle roughly 8 o'clock to 2 o'clock. In this position your rod tip is protected, and you are less likely to hook tree branches. Study your casting position. Is it clear enough to give room for the line as it goes back? Can you land the fish? And, above all, can you get to the proposed position without sending the trout off at a rate of knots, either as a result of your quarry seeing you, or by the scattering of other nearby fish?

When you see a rise form on the surface of a stream, the fish is not likely to be immediately below it. As the trout spots what it imagines to be food, it angles upwards and, depending on the speed of the current, the fish will be carried maybe 2 or 3ft downstream. The rise form will have moved with the current, and so when the fish assumes its original position it could well be 4ft or so upstream of where you thought it would be. These distances are only approximations, but remember to make allowances like this.

Having got to within casting distance, work out sufficient line with several false casts and drop the fly as gently as your skill will allow onto the surface several feet upstream of the last rise.

Make sure that you control the tackle carefully. If the current breaks and a faster run catches the line and drags the fly off course, the fish will usually ignore it. (There are exceptions, as some creatures tend to skate across the surface, but generally speaking it is best to avoid line drag.) A break in the river's flow may be caused by a bank of weed, a sunken log, or an irregularity in the bank. If, however, every time you cast, your fly is going to be pulled off course or made to skid across the surface, you must either find a way to overcome the problem or admit defeat. Apart from being very loath to walk away from a challenge, however, my experience has generally been that fish lying in an awkward position are frequently very good ones, as those in the more easily fished lies are picked off with great regularity. So think twice before you admit defeat. Always consider the options. For example, work upstream to a point at which you can 'feed' the fly down to the fish, keeping plenty of spare or slack line in hand, and making sure that you are in a position to strike immediately the fish takes. Casting from a position directly downstream of the quarry, although feasable, frequently results in replacing the original problem with another. By casting over the fish and dropping the fly

Dapping.

upstream of its lie, you may well just offer the fish a length of line, at which point the game is probably lost.

A cast slanting across and some distance upstream of the fish would allow sufficient time to 'mend' or flick the line into an attitude in which it bowed upstream instead of down. Timing and line control is the essence of the operation, and this, like many other angling skills, is the product of practice and experience. Dapping is another fascinating way of presenting a dry fly and on those occasions where trees and bushes make orthodox casting impossible it is much recommended.

Remember to approach carefully, and while 'dancing' or 'dapping' the fly, be ready to react to whatever demands the hooked fish may make on your tackle. Prepare to give line if necessary – and once the fish is hooked do not worry about breaking cover. It's very doubtful if you will take a second fish from that position.

A 'roll cast' can sometimes be used in cramped conditions, but few seem to employ it. It cannot be practised on grass with any degree of success, but a lake or slow-flowing stretch of river is ideal. First, work out about 10 yards of line, and when it has settled lift the rod tip very slowly to a point above but slightly behind your head. This draws the line towards you and allows an amount of slack or belly to form between the rod tip and the point at which the line touches the water. A smart downwards flick with the rod will send a 'roll' or 'wave' down the line, and the fly is put out to the fish. If you find that you foul the leader when using this cast, try driving the loop slightly to the left. Only practice, or preferably some expert tuition, will help you to perfect this most useful cast.

For the person trying dry fly fishing for the first time I would recommend the simplest of outfits, only adding more sophisticated items in time with increasing experience. I would suggest a glass fibre 8½ or 9ft rod (257 to 272cm) matched with an AFTM 5 DTF line. Glass fibre rods and plastic lines require very little maintenance. They are tough and quite capable of standing up to the hard wear they will get during the learning period.

A complicated reel is not necessary to start with, as for

much of the time fly reels are no more than a receptacle for line not in use. Most fish can be played quite adequately by hand. You will also need a selection of tapered leaders or casts – initially professionally made ones, but learn to tie your own, which will be much cheaper. It is essential to have a variety of leaders, as one with a heavy end helps to present a large fly more efficiently. For example, a big sedge should be tied to about 6lb BS nylon, whereas a much smaller fly would be better if tied to $2\frac{1}{2}$ or 3lb BS monofilament.

Advice on flies should be sought locally, but no doubt any selection would include March Brown, Medium Olive, Greenwells Glory, Tups Indispensable and Black Gnat. Prepare a haversack containing a pair of scissors, penknife, a wallet or similar receptacle for the flies, an amount of Mucillin and a priest to kill your catch before placing into a waterproof bag. (Never leave the catch lying in the sun all day.) You will need a landing net with spring clip or lanyard for easy carrying and no doubt will also want a spring balance to weigh the catch.

Keep your personal clothing equally simple to start with – a pair of polaroid glasses are essential, a hat is advisable, and so is a drab coloured windproof jacket. As for footwear, well, this is a matter of personal choice. Waders are useful but not essential. To start off with I would suggest an ordinary pair of wellingtons.

Chapter 3

Bait

If a bait is to be successful it must be attractive to its quarry, and be used in such a way that it does not prevent the hook from being set when a strike is made. Good baits, like bread, are not necessarily items which would form part of a fish's natural diet. It is also worth noting that it's possible to 'educate' or 'train' certain species into readily accepting a food which would be beyond their natural experience. A good example of this is carp and boiled potato.

Generally speaking, fish accept a bait more willingly if it fits the prevailing circumstances. For example, a small par-boiled potato fished on float tackle capable of supporting the weight, and allowed to drift on the current in a stream full of roach and dace, would not catch many fish. Where there are house-boats and moorings for holiday cruisers, however, it is more than likely that the local population of fish have become used to feeding on waste food regularly dumped overboard. Canned peas, sweetcorn, bacon scraps or any one of a whole range of items could be a successful bait. If the water were relatively still, then a bait fished on the bottom would be taken more readily, but a river calls for a change of style.

Successful angling depends to a very large extent upon the angler's knowledge of the wide range of suitable baits, and also how, where and when to present them. Another important factor is smell and taste, two closely related senses. Fish have the ability to taste and smell a bait and, as explained in chapter 4, they can frequently decide whether or not the offering is to their taste without even taking it into their mouths. Sea anglers frequently use pilchard oil as an appetiser on all manner of baits, and coarse fishermen might add any one of a vast number of flavourings ranging from meat extract to crushed fruit such as bananas and strawberries to paste.

Freshwater baits

Bread is a very popular and versatile coarse fishing bait, and in paste form can be mixed with crushed fruit, cocoa or even beer. Never ignore the possibility that any reasonable additive might tempt an exceptional fish, but do not be too liberal with strong flavours. Obviously there are taints which one should avoid, such as motor oils, nicotine and disinfectants, and I firmly believe that a domestic water supply can sometimes carry sufficient chlorine to make a paste made with it unacceptable to a fish.

Bread can be offered in ways suited to the differing feeding habits of various species and to counteract problems created by environmental conditions. Before illustrating these points, it is absolutely essential to say how important it is that paste can be made correctly. Use water from the river or lake being fished and bread at least three days old. Make the paste in small quantities so that it does not dry out or become sour, and knead it until it reaches an almost cream-like consistency. It should not be so soft that it comes off when cast, but nor should it be a wadding-like pad that prevents the hook being set. Slight pressure with a thumb or finger just above the point can help the hook to penetrate.

A fresh uncut loaf provides flake, an excellent bait for many species, ranging from roach weighing ounces to 20lb carp. Tear it from the white fleshy centre of a loaf and squeeze it around the hook shank, leaving the point just covered by the fluffed-up part of the flake. The outside of the loaf which is used for flake can be cut to provide crust bait. A piece about two inches square with about $1\frac{1}{2}$in of the inner bread still attached can be used as a floating bait for carp fishing. Press the inner part against the outer crust, drive the hook through the crust into the soft part, and then up into the crust. When cast, the flake swells and small pieces gradually break off and float away, acting as an attractor, while the hook remains firmly in the tougher outer part which forms a fairly long-lasting bait.

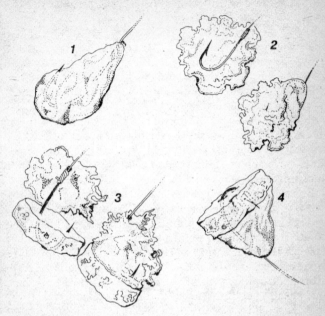

1. Bread paste on hook. 2. Bread flake on hook. 3. Crust with flake before hooking and on hook. 4. Paste on crust (balanced crust).

Crust with some paste squeezed around the hook shank is called balanced crust, and is an excellent bait for laying very lightly on the bottom on a blanket of weed or on mud. The secret is to know how much paste is needed to just balance the crust's buoyancy so that when it absorbs water the whole bait sinks very slowly. Using a crust press – available from most tackle shops – is probably the easiest way of preparing bread-cube baits. These small metal items produce an ideal size bait ready punctured for easy hooking. Push the hook through the crust side first.

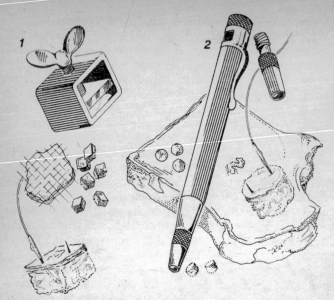

1. Press and bait on hook. 2. Punch and alternative heads with slice of bread.

A slice of bread layed onto a square of hardboard can be used to produce pellets of assorted sizes. A bread punch complete with various heads is a very useful item, as the baits can be cut to a size suited to the hook being used.

Maggots

Although some coarse anglers – mainly those involved in competitive or match fishing – breed their own, the vast majority rely on commercial breeders for their supplies of this very popular bait. There is often some confusion about the names given to maggots – which in the angling sense is normally the larval stage of the blowfly or blue-bottle. But this subject is not a simple one, and in the search for what might be called 'super-maggot' an incredible range of items are used to raise these creatures. Whole chicken, or sometimes just the breast plus various game birds, pigeons, fish, offal and even some cuts of beef are used as the base material on which different flies are allowed to lay their eggs.

Larger or smaller maggots are bred from different types of fly and both temperature and food can have a bearing on whether or not the creature has a soft or tough skin. To make sure that maggots sink when loose fed into the stream as an attractor, they can be grown for a set period, then removed from the food substance and finally fed again a day or so before use, so that they are heavier and therefore sink as required. Such maggots must also be free of grease.

In the northern counties, a maggot known as a 'feeder' becomes a 'squat' further south. A very soft-skinned maggot raised, for example, on chicken, is called a 'gozzer', and another variety, 'pinkies', are bred on fish offal. To the majority of coarse anglers, however, a maggot is just a maggot, and they are content with what is available from the local tackle dealer. Despite the fact that commercially-bred maggots are a perfectly good bait, they can often be made far more effective with a minimal amount of treatment. Maggots purchased in bulk are frequently greasy and they might have an unpleasant odour. They can be improved by laying them on damp sand (an old biscuit tin about three-quarters full) and as they work down through it they clean themselves. Remove any debris left on the surface, and after about 24 hours empty both sand and maggots into a sieve with a mesh suited to holding the maggots but passing the sand. The cleaned maggots can then be left for a further 24 hours or so in bran mixed with a sprinkling of demerara sugar. When taking the prepared baits to the water, store them in a suitable container a half to two-thirds full of bran and sawdust mixed in equal quantities. Most tackle shops stock materials which can be used to dye maggots a variety of colours. A well prepared bait, however, is superior to a greasy smelly one, even if it has got a pronounced colour.

Maggots, if kept long enough and under suitable conditions, turn into chrysalids, or 'casters' as they are usually called by anglers. Casters are an extremely good bait, but their efficiency is frequently impaired through incorrect use. The hook must be well down into the bait (use a long shank hook) because fish will nip at the end and miss being caught.

Before use, always put chrysalids into water. Discard any which float, as these are useless as bait and even worse as a loose feed. Fish congregated by the intelligent use of ground bait can be scattered by casters or greasy maggots going downstream floating on the surface.

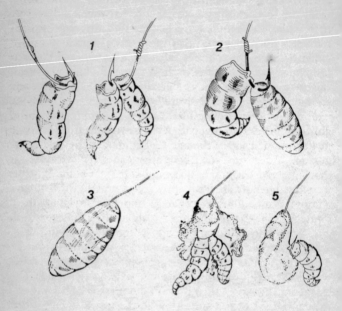

1. Single and double maggot baits. 2. Chrysalis and maggot. 3. Caster. 4. Maggot and bread flake. 5. Maggot and bread paste.

As the diagram shows, it is possible to mix baits, and often these arrangements are very successful. Bee grubs, a new bait which is gradually becoming more easily obtainable, is also an excellent hook bait. During the summer months quite a range of maggots can be found in the countryside, often under cow-pats or in the bark of a rotting log or tree stump. Never ignore what nature offers – they are all possible fish catchers.

Worms and grubs

The ordinary garden worm is an excellent bait, as is the distinctively marked 'brandling'. Both are considerably improved as baits if left for a few days to work through sphagnum moss. Keep the moss damp (just damp – not wet) and do not hold worms in a glass jar with earth and grass in it.

A whole range of small creatures can also be used as bait, often with quite astounding results. Although some of them are freely available, they are frequently ignored by coarse anglers. This is a pity, because if due consideration is given to both presentation and place, these items can be remarkably successful. For example, a caterpillar might be fished on an unshotted line and floated carefully into a stretch of water overhung with trees or bushes. During the summer months chub might well be lying in such a spot, just waiting for small creatures to fall into the water.

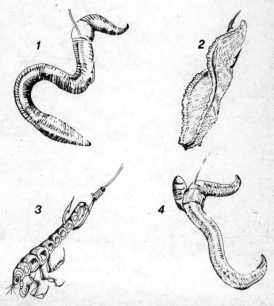

1. Worm on hook. 2. Slug. 3. Caddis grub. 4. Worm and caster.

Woodlice, slugs, water snails and many others can all be tried – but always remember to present them with as much cunning as possible. Consider how these creatures might get into the water, and do your best to present your bait in a similar way.

Grain/seed and pasta

Ready-prepared canned sweetcorn is an excellent bait. In fact, a whole range of grains and seeds including pearl barley, hemp, wheat and rice are used to catch a variety of species. These are not easy baits to fish and hooks size 14 and smaller must be used.

Hemp can be a particularly difficult bait, as it looks similar to split shot. Fish which are used to hemp frequently pick at the shot on the line instead of – and sometimes as well as – the

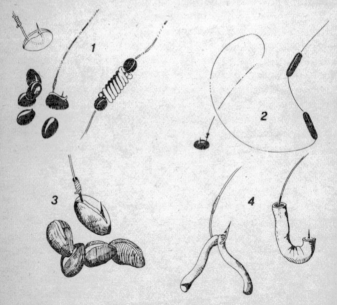

1. Hemp seed on hook with lead wire as weight. 2. Hemp with 'mouse dropping' lead. 3. Wheat on hook. 4. Pasta (macaroni and spaghetti) on hook.

actual bait. This can be overcome by using either an oval-shaped lead or lead wire.

Preparing seeds such as hemp needs some patience, and is frequently only perfected after a period of trial and error. Soak the grains for several hours in cold fresh water, then wash and bring slowly to the boil and simmer. As the grains begin to split and show the white kernel, remove the pan from the heat, drain, and allow to cool slowly. Timing is important when cooking. If the seeds are too hard they cannot be pushed onto the hook and if overcooked they will fall off. Wheat can be treated in a similar way, but experiment with a very small quantity to get the timing right. Different grains need various cooking times.

One of the biggest problems created by using baits of this type is catching large fish on the light tackle and small hooks that must be used. The angler can do no more than be aware of the problem, and consider what might be done in the light of the prevailing circumstances. For example: is the bank clear enough to allow you to follow the fish, and so perhaps avoid some of the additional strain on the line? Is there an area of clear water in which the fish can be played? Is your landing net large enough and is there a spot at which it would be easier to land a specimen? It is surprising how, with care and skill, it is possible to beat a fish of 10 or even 15lb on line of no more than 3lb BS.

Cook pasta in short bait-size pieces. Do not overcook as it will tear off the hook if it is too soft.

Fruit and vegetables
Cherries, blackberries, a piece of apple or a slice of banana, as well as elderberries and blackcurrants, have all at one time or another caught fish. Relate the bait size to the hook, and when using baits of this kind always remember that it is more likely that a fish will accept something which is relatively familiar to it. For example, in waters where silkweed grows, and *only* where it grows, it can be a worthwhile bait. This fluffy weed harbours small creatures and is therefore, from the fish's point of view, something like a larder, and is recognised as a form of food. Collect a clump by hand and

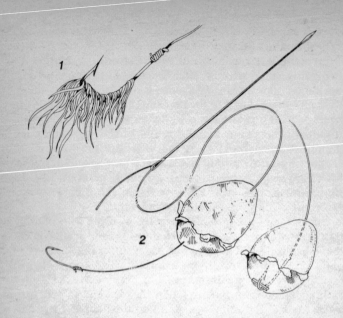

1. Silkweed on hook. 2. Potato on hook with baiting needle.

keep it in water in a plastic bucket or bait container. Wrap portions around a small hook (size 14 or 16) and fish on float tackle for species such as roach and dace.

Potatoes can be a good carp bait, but I would only use egg-sized par-boiled new ones. The diagram here shows how to draw the hook into a potato that has been part skinned. By folding the skin and forming a pad at the bottom, the hook has a cushion against which it presses when cast. This prevents the bait from breaking up. Leave a small patch of skin at the top to help keep the line in position. When cooked, the potatoes should be firm, but not hard. If they are too soft they will fly off the hook, and if too hard the fish will reject them. Use a few dozen very small 'chat' potatoes as ground bait, or larger ones chopped into pieces.

Fish baits

The diagram shows how a variety of dead fish can be used as bait. Both herring and sprats are excellent pike baits and, when costs are a factor, a half pound of sprats is probably one of the cheapest and easiest bait forms of all. They can be bought when available and stored indefinitely in a deep freeze. Frozen sand eels can also be used successfully when fishing for both chub and perch and I have caught pike on them, too.

Frozen sand eels, worked deep and slow, will often lure quite large pike. Before casting, snap the eel in several places, the body will then move more realistically.

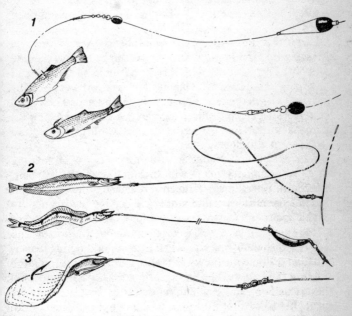

1. *Sprat on float tackle for pike and on leger tackle. 2. Sand eel hooked through the head and fished on a long trail on a paternoster, and a lip-hooked sand eel rigged for spinning. 3. Side of herring on two hooks (tandem). The smaller one is whipped onto a trace to hold the fillet in position.*

Miscellaneous
From time to time notable fish are caught on what some might call unusual baits. These include a slice of sausage or piece of luncheon meat – a variety of cheeses, and sometimes even a cube of fresh tripe or bacon fat.

Cheese – the soft processed type – is a good chub bait – and many a large barbel has been caught on a piece of sausage. Luncheon meat has taken many large carp.

That all these items have lured fish only goes to prove just how catholic their taste can be.

Sea angling baits
Marine worms such as lug, king rag, white rag and red rag are found in various estuaries, harbours and tidal zones of open beaches.

Lug is the most widespread, and it betrays its presence by throwing up sandy mud whirls which can be seen as the tide goes out. Dig carefully with a fork, filling in as you go, and only retain whole worms. Damaged ones go 'off' very quickly and this will kill the rest. Lay them in a wooden bait box lined with newspaper, sprinkle with damp sand and cover with damp sacking. Use them as soon as possible. Lug will not keep for long in hot weather.

White rag is often found in ground similar to that holding lug and although it is not as widespread, it is an excellent bait. Keep it in seawater which must be renewed every six to eight hours. For shorter periods store as lug. King rag is a highly-prized and tough worm. Excellent for fishing as the bait on a baited spoon, it lasts well if kept cool in damp sea sand and covered with damp sacking. The location of king rag beds is usually local knowledge which takes a time to discover. Red rag worm is more usually associated with harbours and estuaries. It is an excellent mullet bait, but is extremely difficult to keep for any appreciable length of time. Both white and red rag worm are primarily associated with shore fishing.

Molluscs
Although seemingly very different, cockles, squid and vari-

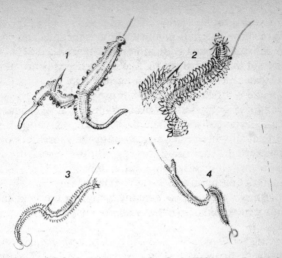

1. Lug worm on hook. 2. King rag on hook. 3. White rag on hook.
4. Red rag on hook.

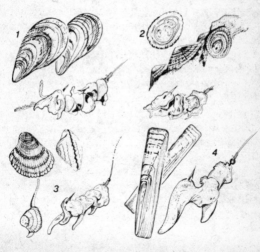

1. Mussel, shell and on hook. 2. Limpet, shell and on hook. 3.
Cockle, shell and on hook. 4. Razor fish, shell and on hook.

ous other molluscs do have similarities and as the diagram here shows, anglers can use many of these as bait.

Mussels are very soft and unless they are part cooked then are not an easy bait to cast. Where casting is not necessary, for example when boat fishing, they are good bait for such species as bream, cod and whiting.

Slipper limpet, either fresh or high, is an excellent bait for bass, flounders and plaice. In some areas great quantities of slipper limpet are thrown up onto the shore by storms. As succeeding tides draw the dead limpets back into the sea, bass and other fish come quite close in to feed. Watch for such conditions and take advantage of them.

Cockles are scraped from the mud, frequently in harbours, but always make sure that you are not taking from an organ-

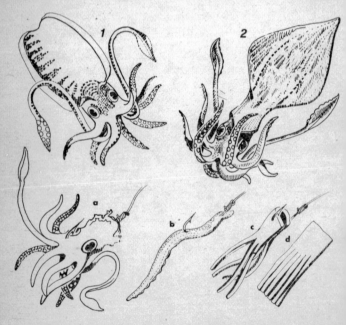

1. Cuttle and (a) the kind of bait it can provide. 2. Squid and (b), (c), (d), different ways of using it as bait.

ised commercial fishery – notice boards will normally be set where there are commercial interests. I do not, however, rate cockles very high as a sea bait.

Razor fish are a good all-round bait, but they are not widely distributed. They live in sandy mud and can be found along the low-water line, sending up fountain-like spurts at intervals. If you are fast enough, you can get a spade under them. Failing that, if you sprinkle salt into the 'blow-hole' the creature will rise.

Two very popular baits are cuttlefish and squid. Cuttlefish are often found dead, floating on the surface out at sea, or even washed up onto the shore. Those thrown up by the tide are usually past being used for bait as the bodies decompose quite quickly. Sea birds also tear them to pieces. One in good condition is a valuable find and can be used in several ways. First, a word of warning: there is an ink-sac in its body and the black fluid in it can cause the most incredible mess. Only clean a squid in a bucket of water, and thoroughly clean the flesh so that the resulting baits are a glistening pearly-white.

Squid, although similar to cuttle, is generally bought from either fishmongers or tackle shops. Whole small squid are excellent baits for cod, tope and large whiting.

Fish baits
Strips, pieces or fillets cut from a variety of species can be used as bait. Mackerel, herring, sprats and sand eel are best, with pouting and bream very much second-line reserves. The diagrams here suggest various ways in which these baits can be prepared and hooked.

The fish which make the best bait forms are either rich in oils and blood – herring, mackerel and sprats – or they are a widely accepted natural food, such as sand eel. Sand eel is an excellent bait for bass, turbot, cod, whiting and many other species. Those baits with a high content of blood and oil are successful because traces of these body juices can be detected by other fish some distance away – certainly further than they can effectively see. Probably the most deadly of all sea angling baits for deep-water boat fishing is really fresh mackerel flesh.

Fish baits and their preparation. 1. Mackerel: whole fish on a Seamaster hook and wire trace. a. Fillet on a tandem hook, b. Strip, c. Cutting and hooking the mackerel last. Herring can be used and prepared in the same way as mackerel. 2. Sprats bunched on a tandem hook. A single hook can be used. 3. Sand eel: a. Hooked through the lower and upper jaws, b. Across and through the eyes, c. Body hooked.

Crustaceans

Although a large number of crustaceans make extremely good baits, the old-time practice of using prawns and shrimps has to a large extent now been made obsolete by both scarcity and sheer value. If there is a chance of turning a single prawn or a few shrimps into one large bass, however, who would say the risk was unjustified?

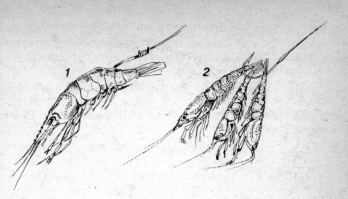

1. Prawn mounted on a single hook. 2. Three shrimps on single hook.

These baits are best fished when casting is unnecessary, such as from a jetty, pier or boat, as they are likely to tear off the hook.

For a crab to grow it is necessary for it to shed its shell, expanding the soft new one it grows before disposing of the old. It then remains in hiding until its new armoured coat has hardened. As the time approaches for it to vacate the old shell, the crab finds a sheltered spot, because during this period it is extremely vulnerable to its hunters. These sanctuaries include thick beds of bladder wrack, under rocks, in fact any odd corner where it feels safe. These are the areas the angler should search for the green back or shore crab that makes such a wonderful bait. Only collect those which are showing signs of being ready to shed their shells, or soft backs if they are going to be used fairly quickly.

The length of time peelers can be held depends entirely on the available storage facilities. In a cool room, packed amid seaweed in a seawater-dampened wooden box and covered with damp sacking they might last a week if the weather was reasonable and a regular supply of fresh seawater was available. Do not overcrowd them, and immediately remove any which die. An old refrigerator provides ideal storage, particularly the salad compartment. Packed in either seaweed or newspaper, it is essential they are kept moist. Domestic supply water can be used in very small amounts, but the crabs must not be ducked in it. The peeling process will be retarded by the lower temperature of the refrigerator, and so watch the baits carefully. Select those which are nearest to the change first, and any which appear to be at the point of dying should either be used at once or, if possible, peeled and frozen.

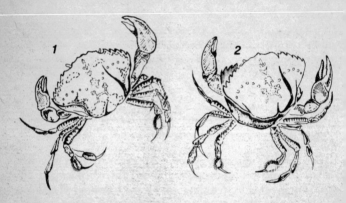

Peeler: 1. Shell starting to lift. 2. Shell almost off.

If these facilities are available, think of ways of using a cool box for storing the baits while fishing. Any unused ones can then be replaced in the 'peeler bank' at the end of the day. Crab bait will tempt a wide variety of fish ranging from the carpet-bag mouth cod and bass to smaller species such as flounder and plaice. The basic formula is simple – large baits for big fish and smaller baits for those with the less capacious mouths. Large fish frequently do take small baits, but in many places one would only expect to catch flounders, plaice and perhaps a few bass to possibly 3 or 4lb. Here the angler should arm his smaller crab baits with a size 1/0 hook. Increase hook size to match the bait but make sure that the point is not masked. When preparing the smaller crab baits, dispense with the lung section.

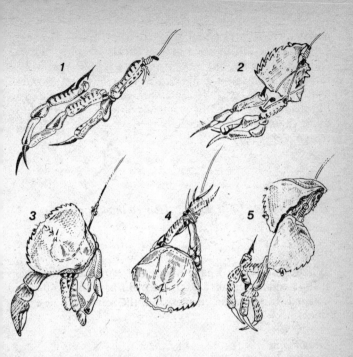

Ways of using crab as bait. 1. Peeled legs. 2. Peeled legs with half or whole body tied around shank and trace line. 3. Peeled crab with one claw removed and hooked. 4. Body hooked and legs bunched and tied around shank. 5. Peeled legs on hook with half body on shank and half body on trace.

Hermit crabs, those odd-shaped creatures which take up residence in empty whelk shells, are also good baits. These are not often found along the shoreline, but are sometimes found clinging to a fish bait reeled in by a boat angler. Professional inshore fishermen, particularly those engaged in lobster potting, are a good source for a supply. Occasionally a ragworm will also be sharing an old whelk shell with a hermit crab.

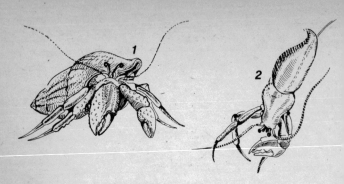

Hermit crab. 1. In its shell. 2. Hooked through its body.

Fish offal
When boat fishing I have frequently caught excellent bags using livers, etc., taken from the fish I have just landed and cleaned. It is a messy business, but the results can be exceptional.

Groundbait
Both freshwater and sea anglers frequently use groundbait to attract fish to the baited hook. A variety of substances and methods are used so that differing situations can be covered. Guidance on particular situations is given in Chapter 5.

Chapter 4

About fish

Fish are highly complex creatures which live in incredibly varied surroundings ranging from shallow streams rushing over rocks to dark oceanic depths. Although certain species such as salmon change their environment and way of life quite dramatically between birth and death, the majority tend to live within fairly well-defined boundaries. Successful angling depends, in no small measure, on the appreciation of these facts, as well as on a basic knowledge of the particular circumstances relating to the various species or groups.

Successful angling is not just a matter of catching fish. Success and full enjoyment of the sport can only be achieved by knowing how to recognise the various species and by being aware of the dangers associated with handling certain fish. Realising the vital importance of treating with care fish which are released after capture is also an essential part of coarse angling. Fish have extremely complicated bodies and their sense organs can so easily be damaged by careless handling. Coarse fish should always be held gently but firmly, the bodies protected by a damp cloth. Take care not to remove too much of their natural coating of slime as this protects them. Never weigh a fish by placing the scale hook into its gills, and always remember that you are responsible for every fish you catch.

If the fish is to be held for a while before being set free, it must be handled correctly, unhooked and retained in a keep-net of suitable size. If it is damaged it will probably die as a result of infection entering the wound. If, however, the fish is to be killed, then it must be done quickly and efficiently. Usually this can be done with a firm blow on the head from a priest (a weighted stick) but larger fish such as conger are dispatched with a sharp-pointed, strong-bladed knife. The spinal cord is severed just to the rear of the head. Never leave a fish to gasp out its life in a polythene bag pushed into a haversack.

There is very little basic difference – except in outward appearance – between the majority of freshwater and marine species. The main external features displayed by fish can be seen in the diagram, but obviously not all species have, for example three dorsal fins, nor do all the fins appear on every species.

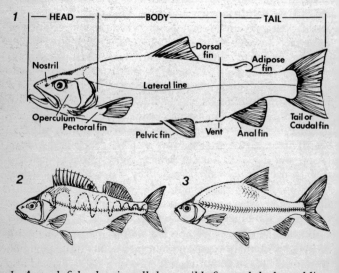

1. A mock fish, showing all the possible fins and the lateral line. 2. Fish with a spiny ray dorsal fin and soft ray dorsal fin. 3. Scale pattern on the lateral line. The scales are counted for identification.

Correct identification can be made by referring to details such as the number of scales along the lateral line, the number of rays in a particular fin or perhaps the positioning of the fins. Body colour and specific marking also help identification.

1. Thumb print on the shoulder of a John Dory. 2. Thumb prints on a haddock. 3. Bars on the flank of a perch. 4. Wing markings on a cuckoo ray. 5. Wing markings on a sandy ray.

It is fascinating to note how the various markings help fish to blend with their usual surroundings, a fact quite common in nature. The positioning and size of a fish's eyes is also important. They complement the creature's way of life. Nowhere is this fact more apparent than in the pike, which lurks in the shelter of cover waiting to flash out and seize its prey. It is also interesting to compare the size and position of the eyes of tench and pike. Tench feed mainly on the bottom where their rooting would create muddy conditions, whereas pike depend to a large extent on being able to see their prey.

1. Pike. 2. Tench.

Note the way the pike's dorsal, caudal and anal fins are grouped. This helps the fish to produce rapid acceleration, enabling it to catch its food. The angler must also realise that fish's vision isn't only forward and down through water. They are perfectly capable of spotting the careless angler, especially if he is a silhouette against the sky.

By swinging its tail or caudal fin from side to side, a fish moves forward. Other manoeuvres are achieved by manipulating the various fins.

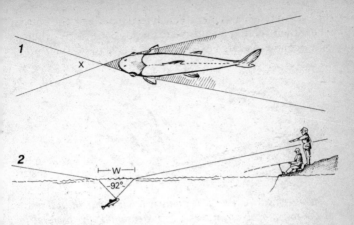

Fish vision. 1. The fish has a small area of lost vision in front and in the areas along its flanks. A morsel of food at X will be in a binocular field. 2. The fish has upward vision through a cone of approximately 92 degrees. The window W is circular and increases in size as the fish descends. It is well to keep a low profile on the waterside.

It isn't always necessary for a fish to keep swimming in order to maintain its position. Most are equipped with a swim bladder, an internal bag-like organ filled with gas which gives the body the amount of buoyancy necessary to keep it at a constant depth. Some species have a relatively simple bladder, others have a system which is quite complicated. Fish accustomed to living in deep water such as pollack, which can be found around a reef 100ft or so down, die as a result of being brought rapidly to the surface. The swim bladder bursts. Species such as shark and mackerel which do not have swim bladders are capable of going deep and then returning rapidly to the surface.

Although there is a fairly clear demarcation line between many salt and freshwater species, there are some which are able to tolerate, to a greater or lesser extent, the opposite conditions to which they are normally accustomed. Pike, for example, can live in brackish water, and the minnow is found

Fish movement. 1. The heavy muscle formation in the tail section of the fish propels it forward. 2. Extension of the pectoral fin, together with caudal or tailfin movement, will turn the fish to left or right. 3. Inflation or deflation of the internally positioned swim-bladder – used in a similar way to a submarine's ballast tanks – will cause the fish to rise or sink in the water. This action may well be coupled with the use of angled pectoral fins which will act in a similar way to a submarine's hydroplanes.

in a similar situation in the Baltic. Bass seem able to penetrate quite a distance into the lower reaches of some rivers, and mullet have been caught in rivers as far as 20 miles from the sea. Flounders provide yet another example.

The reasons why certain species can adapt quite quickly to major changes in the level of salinity are both various and complex. Briefly, those living entirely in freshwater never drink. They absorb all the water they need through their mouths and gill membranes, and their very efficient kidneys filter out whatever excess there might be. Marine fish loose water from their system, sucked out by osmosis, and so they have to drink. As a result of swallowing seawater they have a build-up of salt which has to be filtered out by their kidneys. The salt is then ejected from their bodies. So there is a very fundamental difference between freshwater and marine fish and any species capable of making the complete transition from salt to freshwater, or vice-versa, must be able to adjust its organs and bodily functions to fully accommodate both conditions. Very few have this ability, but those which have include salmon, eels and flounders. Those which have a limited capability include bass and sticklebacks.

Species like salmon which are born in freshwater, but migrate seawards, returning to freshwater to spawn are termed 'anadromous'. Those like the eel which go back to the sea to spawn after a life in freshwater are termed 'catadromous'.

Apart from these very basic divisions, there are many other reasons why fish tend to congregate in certain areas. They seek and colonise those parts offering conditions which may, for example, complement their body shape, or provide the type of environment which holds the sort of food essential to their survival. This applies to both freshwater and sea fish. The great slab-sided bream would not last long in the hurly-burly of a boulder-filled moorland stream. The force of the current, acting as a continuous pressure on its body, would rapidly exhaust the creature, and its food supply would be minimal or non-existent. Another important factor is oxygen. Species such as trout and perch need far more than, say, carp and tench. And so the general picture begins to build up of the various species which have similar needs colonising those stretches of river which provide what is essential to their way of life.

Sea fish tend to congregate in certain areas, too. The reasons for this range from the fact that some choose particular areas for spawning while others come and go as part of a migratory process. There are also some which select and stay in one place because it provides both a sufficiency of food and a secure hideaway.

Black bream are a good example of a species which congregates each year for spawning. Marks off the Sussex, Hampshire and Dorset coast are well known for this fact. Spur dog migrate in huge packs, moving between their summer feeding areas and overwintering zones with great regularity. Conger are well known for their habit of taking up residence in a wreck or rocky fissure. From there they sally forth to feed on smaller fish which also inhabit such places.

Typical distribution of fish in a river ranging from salmon and trout in cold, well aerated high country streams to esturial waters where bass and flounders live.

120

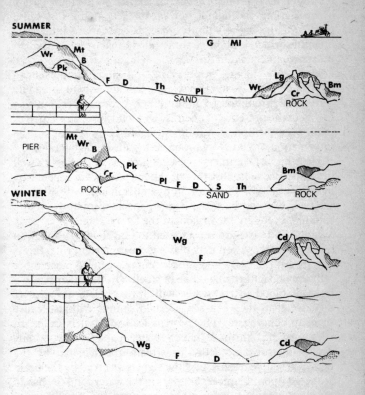

In coastal waters changes in water temperature can cause fish migration. The two diagrams show possible changes in the fish populations from summer to winter. (B-bass, Bm-bream, Cd-cod, Cr-conger, D-dab, E-eel, F-flounder, G-garfish, Lg-ling, Ml-mackerel, Mt-mullet, Pg-pouting, Pl-plaice, S-sole, Th-thornback, Wg-whiting, Wr-wrasse.)

Information about fish behaviour is a vital ingredient of successful angling.

The senses

Although used as one of several reference points for accurate identification, the lateral line is, in fact, a series of sense organs of the highest importance. It consists of numerous openings which lead into a slime-filled canal which, although most prominent along the sides, extend onto the head. These organs sense changes in pressure, and the messages sent to the brain via this system enable the fish not only to thread its way safely through fast-running, rock-strewn water, but also to detect the presence of enemies and food. Predators such as pike, even if blind, can hunt successfully by relying on the information provided by the sense organs in the lateral line.

Hearing is another sense which is extremely well developed in fish, and the vibrations which are created by heavy footfalls on the bank, or by knocking the side of a boat are picked up by both the hearing mechanism and – if at a suitable level – by the organs in the lateral line.

Smell and taste are senses used to find food. Although in some predators vision may play a more important role, this is not always the case. Pike, for example, seem to place more reliance on sight than a sense of smell. On the other hand, a trace of blood in the water will draw shark a far greater distance than they can see. Certain sounds will also cause them to congregate. The nostrils lead to what is called an 'olfactory pit' through which water passes. Any odour-producing substances in this stream are detected by the highly-sensitive organs, and the signals received by the brain are acted upon. Unpleasant taints in the water send the fish to more acceptable surroundings, but attractive smells entice the fish to investigate more closely.

The taste buds are particularly important to fish who feed at night and where vision can be strictly limited by conditions.

This is in no way a comprehensive account of the senses which fish possess but it does serve to give the angler a series of valid reasons why certain actions should or should not be taken. Make an open and noisy approach to the waterside and you may well kill any chance you had of catching fish. Remember that it is possible for them not only to see you

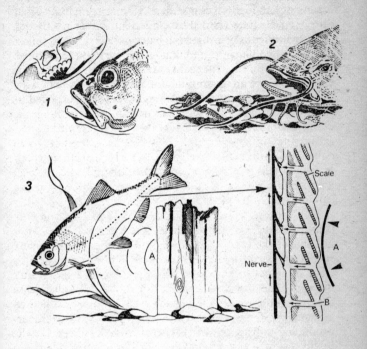

Sensory organs. 1. The nostrils and olfactory pit. The track followed by water passing through the pit is indicated. The information is carried from the organ to the brain. 2. Sensory barbels and other taste buds. The barbels are covered with extremely sensitive taste buds and are used to locate food. Taste buds can also be in the mouth and elsewhere. 3. The lateral line. This is formed by a collecton of external openings to a fluid-filled canal (B). Changes in pressure caused by the close proximity of an obstacle or vibrations (A) caused by a heavy foot on the bank vary the pressure in the canal. These changes are picked up by nerve endings and are transmitted to the brain.

arrive, but also to feel and hear you. Fish that have been undisturbed for six days do not take kindly to a noisy invasion on the seventh.

Although the sea is a vast area, and it may seem impossible for a relatively infinitesimal bait to contain sufficient oils and juices to attract fish, using fresh baits and good presentation does pay big dividends. Think how far, even in the polluted atmosphere of a city, the scent of frying bacon will carry. In this instance we are comparing the nose of urban man with that of a wild creature whose senses have been sharpened to enable its species to survive aeons of time.

Chapter 5

In which we go fishing

There is no magic combination of bait, tackle and method which unerringly catches the species of one's choice. If there were, angling would immediately lose much of its fascination. But one thing is certain, the unexpected can, and frequently does, occur. This does not mean that a line cast with little more than hope is the answer. There should always be a basic pattern to one's fishing, a design to which the individual adds his own refinements which come from knowledge gained through expanding experience of local conditions. But with some overlap between both the zones occupied by particular species and their lifestyles, it is obvious that similar tackle and tactics will frequently take different species. Selective fishing is always possible, but the degree to which it is successful depends not only upon the variety of species in a particular fishery, but also on the ability of the angler to follow basic guidelines.

Distribution and habits

These gregarious and powerful river fish, although not widely distributed, are one of the most important of all our freshwater species. They can tax the angler's skill more than most, and the lessons learned while fishing for them can be put to great use when angling for most other species.

Barbel are a bottom feeding variety which only seem to thrive in rivers offering a generally moderate temperature, a reasonable flow and areas of gravel and stone over which they tend to congregate. Rivers noted for their stocks of barbel

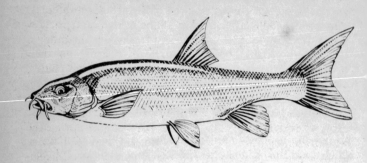

Scale count: LL 55—65. Inferior mouth. Two pairs of sensory barbels on upper lip. British Record: 13lb 12oz (6K 237gm). Although correct at the time of writing, changes occur from time to time. The figures quoted in this chapter should provide an indication of the weight the species can achieve.

include the Dorset Stour, Hampshire Avon, Thames, Swale, Severn and Trent, but even in these rivers they are not evenly spaced. There are several features which appear to be common to those places where barbel shoal. Their preference for gravel and stone has already been mentioned, but they also like to be near weed where they can find a variety of food. The fish tend to lie quite close together, and usually at a spot where the current brings food.

A shoal also seems to develop what might be called a 'pecking order', with those at the head of the 'pack' moving to the rear as soon as they have taken what they need from whatever supply is available. This can have a bearing on the method of angling, and it also means that the spot which produces the first fish might well yield several more. The importance of this should not be forgotten.

Barbel also lie in what can be called 'sheltered' spots such as a depression in the river bed, in the quieter water at the end of a run, or behind a boulder. Once again, these are places where items of food might be dropped by a slackening current. But they do not shun the most powerful streams, having an ideal shape for combatting the most turbulent water. At dusk on very dull days barbel might be seen in quite shallow water, foraging for insect larvae and freshwater shrimps.

Temperature has quite a significant bearing on their behaviour. They become more lethargic as it grows colder, and a sharp drop in water temperature will stop them feeding altogether. As the temperature rises again they often feed quite furiously, and that's a time when you may take the catch of a lifetime. Although barbel are caught during the winter months, they are certainly not eager to feed. Once again it is, I believe, a matter of water temperature. A relatively mild spell with some rain from the west can produce worthwhile conditions, but an inflow of water from melting snow or a period of cold easterly winds will rapidly put the barbel off.

Tackle, methods and bait

Use a powerful bottom rod for float fishing, or an equally robust leger rod, a reel filled with 6lb BS line, and a selection of hooks between size 4 and 10. Although there are occasions when lighter floats can be used, the Avon and ducker type are most often called for because stronger tackle and heavier shotting is needed to combat the conditions in the generally faster rivers in which barbel live.

Set the float to give about 8 to 12in more line between hook and float than there is depth of water. Place the bulk of the shot fairly low down so that, when cast, it travels downstream just above the river bed. This will keep the bait right on the bottom where the barbel feeds. As the float goes downstream, hold it back with a light pressure on the outflowing line. Brake carefully and steadily, not in jerks, as this will only cause the bait to rise and swing erratically.

At the end of each 'trot-down' hold the line firmly for a moment or two. The current will then lift the bait off the bottom before tackle recovery is started. If possible, swing the rod tip in such a way that the float is drawn back along a different path to the one taken while going downstream. This helps to cut down the amount of disturbance in the swim being fished. Present the bait in a run between weed beds, or into a very turbulent stretch of water. Let the current take the bait and remember that the fish might be lying at the edge of the faster water, waiting for the stream to bring the food to them.

Float fishing can be the most efficient method during cold weather because the fish will be less active, and bait moving to them might well be more attractive than one presented on a static leger. Although barbel have been caught on a size 6 hook baited with a single grain of sweetcorn, I do not favour small baits fished on small hooks and light line is not for me. All too often these powerful fish are able to break free, leaving them with hook-decorated lips, and trailing lengths of nylon. Barbel are not what I would call 'hook-shy' fish. They are bold rumbustuous creatures that normally leave the angler in no doubt that one has taken the bait.

When the float dips, strike against the run of the fish and be prepared to give line. Keep the rod tip up, and if the tension on the reel spool is set correctly, this braking effect will soon turn the fish, at which point you start regaining line. Keep in touch with the fish. Never allow slack line to accumulate, and never reel in while the fish is drawing line, this will only increase strain unnecessarily, and impart some twist into the line. As the fish weakens, draw it in carefully but be prepared for a last rush. Sink the landing net, coax the fish over it and lift. Never, repeat never, chase a fish with the landing net. If the fish cannot be drawn over the net, it is still too lively to be landed.

Barbel have a particularly catholic taste, and so most recognised baits, plus many which are unusual, will tempt them. However, most noted barbel fisheries have what might be called a 'popular' or 'favourite'. Baits become popular on particular fisheries because they are used to such an extent that the fish begin to accept the item as a regular part of their diet. For example, Joe Smith may well take a noteable bag whilst baiting with a piece of beef sausage and this news will spread like wildfire. Within days, beef sausage will appear as a regular item on the diet of fish in that water, and inevitably more catches will be made. It isn't long before beef sausage becomes 'the' bait to use, and yet another fashion is born. One only has to look at the list of one-time 'killer' baits to see how fashions change. Who today uses greaves, pith, or boiled bullocks brains, baits which were highly regarded before the turn of the century?

Apart from those items which might be called 'fishery specialities', barbel can be tempted by most recognised coarse fish baits. Maggots are excellent but so is bread in various forms, such as paste and flake. Worm is one of my favourite offerings, especially after the first really heavy autumnal rains, but I never use just one. When fishing worm for barbel, use a size 4 or 6 hook holding several lively well scoured lobs or brandlings.

Legering is another popular method, some would say the best. Accurate casting can place baits into locations which may well be unreachable with a float. A leger rod, quiver tip and swimfeeder/leger rig is one style, but the swimfeeder must contain samples of the hook bait. Pack the swimfeeder with crumb mixed with pellets of cheese, chopped worm or maggots – whatever is being used on the hook. When setting up a legering situation it is by far the easiest if you cast downstream to the fish. Sit opposite the target area or downstream of it, and your problems are greatly increased.

Select the lead which is just heavy enough to hold in the chosen position. If necesary it can be 'hopped' downstream by tightening the line – lifting the rod tip – and then paying out a few feet of line until the weight settles once again. If circumstances force you to fish across or upstream, the tackle must be carefully balanced. Choose a lead which will almost, but not quite, hold the baited hook in position. Then add a large split shot to the line some 4 to 6in from the hook. This additional weight should be sufficient to hold the tackle in position. When cast in, the line is adjusted, and when set up on rod rests the rod tip will normally assume a downward tilt. As the fish takes the bait, the line will slacken and the rod tip lift. Watch for this to occur and, as it does, strike. This is usually referred to as a 'drop back' bite.

A clear, snag-free run can be fished with a rolling leger. Cast out across the stream and, once the terminal tackle has settled, check the outflow of the line and recover the excess. Keep in touch with the lead and learn to feel the various movements it makes as the current swings it around and across the area being fished. I always hold a loop of line between left thumb and forefinger while holding the rod in my right hand. The line is pulled down to form a 'V' between reel and bottom ring, and the line carries every vibration created by the weight as it 'rumbles' over the river bed. A little experience and some practice will soon provide the necessary expertise. And the first bite – although you may miss it – will be one sensation you will never forget.

When fishing a rolling leger, you will find it advantageous to use baits which stay on the hook well, such as worm and maggot. Bread flake does not last well while being swept over stony ground by turbulent water.

Groundbait

Basically, ground bait is used to congregate fish into a set area, encourage them to feed, and to hold their interest while you catch them. This means the feed must be placed in exactly the right position and consist wholly or partly of whatever is being used as hook bait. It must also be delivered in a quantity that will keep their interest while not overfeeding them. It is amazing how many just distribute at random vast quantities of maggot, and then use either worm or bread as a hook bait.

Barbel feed on the bottom, so the ground bait must be offered there. If it is to be effective, the feed must follow the line taken by the baited hook. If you are using maggot as a hook bait, greasy ones floating on the surface will not help, neither will floating casters. A bait-dropper can assist in placing a supply of ground feed in the correct position, and it might also help to encase a number of maggots within a ball of well-dampened breadcrumb, or some suitably prepared proprietary brand groundbait mixture.

The same thing applies to whatever hook bait is being used. Assuming that it is not possible to feed the swim entirely with a suitable quantity of whatever is being placed on the hook, samples of it must be added to the groundbait mixture.

BREAM
Abramis brama

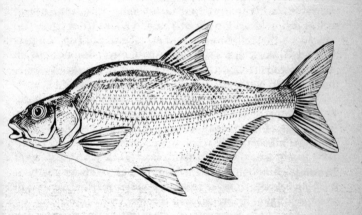

Scale count: LL 51–60. Anal fin. 24–30 branched rays, strongly concave. (Silver bream, Blicca bjoerkna, scale count: 44–48. Anal fin 21–30 rays.) British record 13lb 8oz (6K 123gm).

Distribution and habits

Bream is a fish of both river and lake which is widely distributed throughout the British Isles. They are a shoaling species which favour areas offering muddy beds where they root for the worms, crustacea and larvae which form a major part of their diet.

In rivers, the shoals would be expected to inhabit sections with deep water and the most sluggish current. Bream do not have a physical shape suited to fast, streamy runs and they would rapidly become exhausted by the effort of combating the current.

Bream give sport throughout the season, but the colder the weather the greater is their tendency to congregate in the deepest and most sheltered water they can find. They are interesting fish to catch, but as fighters they are more heavy than active.

Tackle, methods and bait

Use standard bottom rod for float fishing, or a similar leger rod, a reel holding 3 to 4lb BS line and hooks from sizes 10 to 16, depending on both bait and average size of fish. Anglers often use hooks larger than they should, for although bream are a bulky fish, they have a relatively small mouth. A size 16 hook baited with a single maggot or caster will be more successful than larger hooks and baits, particularly on hard-fished water.

Although bream are, in essence, a bottom feeding species, they will take baits fished higher in the water. A broad deep river can be fished with orthodox float tackle with the float set to present the bait either just on or slightly above the bed. Fishing 'on the drop' is another popular method, as bream may well 'take' before the bait reaches the bottom.

The fish often congregate in what is called a 'bream hole', an extra deep section where a slackening current drops food items. Here, the technique described as 'laying-on' can be used. A bite is first signalled by the float laying flat. The lift method can also be used where the current is very slack. A bream's shape means that when feeding it must almost stand on its head, so the lift method will work quite efficiently, but remember to strike as the float rises. This is a style which is even more successful when fishing still water.

Legering is a time-honoured bream fishing method, and either a quiver or swing-tip style used in conjunction with a swimfeeder or link leger is ideal. I prefer a quiver tip and, in deep water with a reasonable flow, a swimfeeder/leger. The current washes the groundfeed out and spreads it to attract the fish. Where the stream is negligible, a link leger with groundbait distributed by hand is more reliable.

When circumstances force you to cast to the limit of your range, a paternoster rig will help prevent the terminal tackle from tangling in flight. The weight can be an Arlesey bomb – a swimfeeder would probably be too ungainly to achieve the necessary distance. A throwing stick or catapult will help to deliver the groundbait.

When handling bream for the first time you will find that its body is covered with a heavy coating of slime. Handle it with great care, holding the fish in a damp cloth, and remember that the slime is the creature's first line of defence against disease.

Bread in various forms, such as cube, flake and paste, are excellent baits, particularly during the summer months when maggot and worm attract the eel population which are almost invariably found in lakes and rivers holding bream. However, as a moving bait is not as likely to attract eels as frequently as a stationary one, maggots can be tried when 'trotting', but I would advise against a worm bait until the colder weather. During the summer I prefer casters to maggots. Worms are a deadly eel bait during the summer months, wait until the lower temperatures send eels into hiding in their winter quarters before using worms for bream fishing.

Groundbait
Bream will consume quite massive amounts of groundbait, but always remember that your main objective is to attract and hold their interest, not provide a feast. Indiscriminate groundbaiting with tens of pounds of feed is not as effective as the regular handful placed in the right spot. Always include samples of the hook bait, and if using balls of dampened rusk or crumb, do not forget to allow for the downstream drift caused by the current.

CARP
Cyprinus carpio

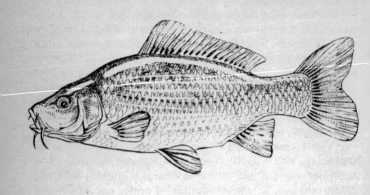

Scale count: LL 33–40. Four barbels, two on long corner of mouth, two on short upper lip. British record 44lb (19K 957gm).

Distribution and habits

The common carp has two mutations, mirror and leather and, apart from pike, there are no species of coarse fish of comparable size generally available to the British angler. Of the three varieties, only the common carp is fully scaled. The mirror has one or two rows along the lateral line, and possibly a few large scales on the top of the back, on either side and forward of the dorsal fin. Leather carp are virtually without scales and the skin is tough and leathery, hence its name. There can be scattered patches of scales.

All three varieties are widely distributed in areas where there are still waters and very sluggish rivers which offer a good growth of weed and mud and/or gravel beds which the fish can dredge for insect larvae and worms. They also take snails and other creatures which they may find on water plants and on the underside of lily pads.

Temperature has a vital influence on these fish, and generally the angler's chances of catching one diminishes quite rapidly as the water temperature either falls below about 15°C (60°F) or goes above 21°C (70°F). Where there are special circumstances, such as a water fed by a spring which has a constant and acceptable temperature, or an inflow of warmed water from a manufacturing plant, carp often become accustomed to them and remain active throughout the winter. But these are special factors which lead carp to move away from their more usual pattern of peak summer activity, slowing down during the autumn, lying mainly dormant in winter, to become active once again as the temperature rises in the spring.

Although carp certainly feed and are caught during the middle of the day in the sun's full glare, my experience has been that the periods from sunset to midnight, and from about one hour before dawn until the sun first strikes the water, are the times most likely to produce results. Warm but overcast days have also been notable occasions. Although carp are caught in some rivers, serious or specialist carp fishing is basically a stillwater sport.

Because the carp is, in many ways, a rather unique creature, fishing for them involves a considerable amount of study. This does not necessarily mean a study in the widest sense, but rather a detailed one concerning the particular water you fish. The problems facing the angler include locating the feeding areas favoured by the carp and discovering the baits they will take. For example, they will often feed on the shelving banks leading to the margin weed. Usually they shun these areas if there is any unusual activity, but as it gets darker they will move closer to the shoreline. There may well be shallows and clumps of reeds, or patches of lily some distance off-shore, trees or bushes overhanging an inaccessible bay with a shelving bed. These are areas where carp feed, but it may take weeks or even several seasons of careful study and observation to discover the vital facts about the water you fish.

When the feeding zones are found, the problem of baits still remains. Frequently bread, in one of its many forms, can be the most generally successful. Paste can be flavoured with cheese, meat extracts, tinned fish or liver sausage. It is also possible to make up various concoctions based on ordinary flour or different cereals – the permutations are endless. The main fact to remember is that carp can associate various items with an unpleasant experience, such as being hooked. And herein lies yet another problem, because, as a result of their experiences, carp can easily change their feeding pattern and, in so doing, send the angler back to square one.

Carp fishing is an intriguing game, but it's a slow one. It can easily take a couple of seasons of really intensive fishing before the first double-figure carp takes your bait, and even then there is a long way to go before it is brought to the net.

Tackle, methods and bait

Ideally, use a specialist carp rod, or one capable of dealing effectively with the size of fish you might reasonably expect to catch. This is an important point because often various waters tend to hold fish which fit into a certain size range. Some may yield 25 and even 30lb fish with fair regularity, while in other waters the average size of carp may be between 5 and 10lb. It is pointless using tackle designed to subdue 35 or even 40lb carp if you are fishing a canal or lake holding predominantly 5 to 7 pounders. So use tackle suited to local conditions.

In average conditions a rod matched to an 8 to 10lb BS line would be ideal, plus a selection of hooks, floats and weights to match the baits and styles of fishing. There are two items, the landing and keep-net, which must be special. The average nets are just not capable of holding large carp. Before attempting this type of coarse fishing, either equip yourself correctly or accompany someone who has an adequate landing net. On the other hand there is no need to worry unduly about a keep-net, as I believe carp should be released immediately they are unhooked – and photographed if necessary. If they are held, use a large keep-net or a big, open weave sack held apart by a 'former'. This can be used to retain the fish for a while if it is vital, but make sure that the fish is in water deep enough for its comfort, and that the net does not lie on its body.

The majority of carp are taken on the simplest of leger tackle, frequently no more than a hook tied direct to the reel line, with bait a size and type (such as a potato or large piece of paste) to provide sufficient casting weight. Fishing over a very soft bed can be helped by using a balanced crust bait. If a lighter bait is used, then select a leger rig with a weight, but still one offering the least complications. This also applies if additional weight is required to facilitate longer casting.

Margin fishing with floating crust is another extremely successful style, but the utmost caution is essential as the bait is just a rod-length away from the angler. The implications of this are obvious: movement and the vibrations it would create would rapidly destroy any chance of enticing a fish. When using this method make sure that the line will flow freely once the bait has been taken. Any resistance would probably result in the fish dropping the bait immediately and so the rod must be set up carefully and supported on two rests, the tip out over the water just clear of the reeds. Keep the crust floating close in to the reeds and make sure that no excess line is allowed to spill onto the surface.

Legering, or margin fishing with floating crust, call for a very delicate method of bite detection. A carp of any appreciable size will frequently 'run' quite a distance immediately it has taken a bait, so the bite detector must not impede the outflow of line. Carp fishers employ a number of indicators, ranging from battery-powered items, which give both sight and sound warning, to luminous bobs and rolls of silver foil on the line.

Float fishing techniques do catch some carp, but it is not a style which I would choose. Apart from the resistance offered by the float and, to some extent, the split shot, there is the problem of actually seeing the float after dark. As I have already said, serious carp fishing tends to be an after-dusk or pre-dawn exercise, and one which includes an enormous amount of waiting.

When the long-awaited bite does materialise, you may find that the fish is not acting as you expected. Floating crust is often taken quite deliberately, and the line will start running out in the usual way. At this point you strike and set the hook. Carp are powerful fish, and it is useless to try to hurry a big one. Keep the rod tip up and make the fish fight for every inch of line it takes. Let it tire itself against the spring in the rod and the spool tension.

If it gets into a weed bed it may be possible to wade out to clear it or you may have to wait until the fish swims away of its own accord. It may react to either steady and continuous strain, or sometimes a completely slack line will do the trick. On some occasions I have brought a carp out from a weed bed with a few well-aimed balls of groundbait.

There are times when carp seem unable to make up their mind, and virtually all the indication you get of a bite is a 'twitch' or 'pluck' on the line. On other occasions the take can be very slow, but certainly more positive, although the fish may only take a foot or so of line, causing the indicator to rise perhaps no more than a few inches. The only countermove that I have ever found to be relatively successful has demanded complete concentration. I watch the line as intently as possible and strike as the indicator starts to move.

I have already mentioned the multiplicity of baits that can be used for carp fishing, but do not forget the importance of the hook the bait conceals. Select one which is not only complimentary to the bait's size, but one that has been carefully honed and in peak condition. Consider the thickness of the wire too. A super-sharp fine wire hook will penetrate and hold the fish on the strongest section, the bottom of the bend. A hook which is well set into a carp's tough jaw will give you the best possible chance of success. In waters where the fish are, on average, what can reasonably be called small, say 4 to 7lb, a line of 4lb BS with size 8 to 12 hooks can be adequate.

Scale up the tackle to suit the fish you can reasonably expect to catch. Remember, there is nothing sporting in losing a fish as a result of using tackle that should not have been employed in the first place. My earlier remarks about barbel with 'hook-decorated lips' apply equally to carp.

Groundbait

This is an important aspect of carp fishing, but take care not to over-bait. Ideally, you should be able to work to a plan which will not be interrupted by the activities of other anglers, but there are very few who enjoy such a privilege. If it is possible, feed the area surrounding the point you intend placing your bait with either a proprietary brand of groundbait or your own mixture, but once again remember how important it is to include samples of whatever you intend using on the hook.

The general scheme I adopt is to place the lightest possible scattering of feed out on the perimeter of the bait target area, gradually increasing the amount as one gets towards the centre. It is quite simply a matter of trying to entice the fish in towards the point where the baited hook will be. If possible, feed the area for two or three weeks.

Needless to say, most anglers have to accept the fact that others also use not only the same lake, but also the same swim. In this case, try to capitalise on the groundbait others will have put in before you arrived. Only feed lightly and, above all, do not bombard a likely feeding area with great clods of groundbait and then expect to catch fish. You might, but you are certainly stacking the odds against yourself.

Finally, remember that the best carp fishing months are the ones in which eels are most active. If you groundbait with particles of worm or quantities of maggot you will inevitably attract eels. If you use either worm or maggot as hook bait, you must also expect to catch eels far more regularly than carp.

CARP (Crucian)
Carassius Carassius

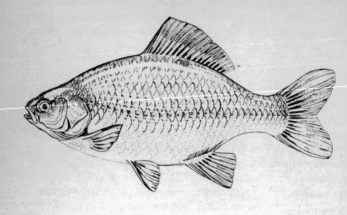

*Scale count: LL 31–36. Barbels absent. Dorsal fin strongly
convex. British record 5lb 10oz 5dr (2K 565gm).*

Distribution and habits

Although this species has an overall distribution similar to
common carp, it is not found in as many waters. They favour
an environment with plenty of weed, plus a bed which they
can sift for the worms and other small creatures which form
the basis of their diet. Temperature is important and crucian
carp follow the pattern set by the common and its mutations.

Tackle, methods and bait

Crucian carp can be taken by similar methods to those used
when fishing for other members of the carp family, but pay
due regard to their size and scale the tackle down accordingly.

CATFISH (Wels)
Silurus glanis

Broad head and mouth. Three pairs of barbels, one long pair on upper lip, two short pairs on lower lip. British record 43lb 8oz (19K 730gm).

Distribution and habits
These quite unusual looking fish have a very limited distribution, mainly in the eastern counties. The movement of catfish is resisted by RWA fishery departments, and generally they are not a popular fish with anglers, despite their size. They are basically bottom feeding creatures which are more active at night.

Tackle, methods and bait
Generally, use leger tackle and methods, baits include dead fish.

CHUB
Leuciscus cephalus

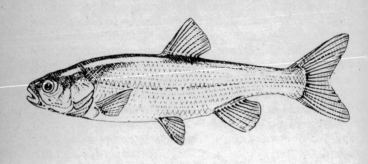

Scale count: LL 44–46. Dorsal and anal fin with convex free edge. British record 7lb 6oz (3K 345gm).

Distribution and habits

Except for northern Scotland, west Wales and south-west England, chub are a widely distributed river species. In some streams, particularly the small ones, chub of surprisingly large proportions are sometimes found inhabiting deeper pockets of water where overhanging bushes and trees give additional cover. Although a shoaling fish, chub seldom act in unison, except when threatened by danger.

They will take a wide range of baits, and can be caught during the blazing heat of high summer as well as when the rivers begin to freeze along the margins. Chub are not a fish of predictable habits. On one occasion they may take a legered lob worm with great gusto, but within days, and under identical conditions, the only way to catch them may be two yellow maggots on a size 14 hook fished on float tackle.

They are one of the most challenging species to fish for and can offer resistance out of all proportion to their size.

Tackle, methods and bait

Although specialised tackle is not particularly essential, a good working knowledge of the many styles of coarse fishing is necessary. The essence of successful chub fishing lies in the angler's ability to present his bait both accurately and in a way that will attract the chub's attention. Your basic tackle should include a standard bottom or ledger rod matched with line ranging from 3 to 5lb BS plus a selection of floats, weights and hooks from size 8 to 14.

Before attempting to fish, it is wise to assume that a noisy approach, or movement outlined against the sky will result in scaring all the chub in the vicinity. There are few fish that react more positively to anything even remotely resembling danger. In fact, having taken a brace from one stance, you may well have to move or present your bait elsewhere before catching another.

At the beginning of the season chub are frequently found in faster, well aerated water, just the situations favoured by barbel. Similar tactics will catch them, but when chub fishing do not stick rigidly to presenting the bait right on the bottom. They will feed at virtually any level, but remember that it's important for the baited hook to precede the float. When fishing more turbulent streams this is not so essential. When 'long trotting', a fluted float will tend to hold its course more accurately, even when there are side pressures exerted by the line which may need 'mending' from time to time.

There's rarely any doubt that a chub has taken your bait. As the float dips, tighten the line immediately, but keep the rod tip up. With the clutch set correctly, the first powerful plunge should be held with ease, but also with caution. Regain line as soon as you can. This removes the fish from its fellows and causes the least disturbance in the swim. It also draws the fish into clearer water which is particularly important as chub have a habit of diving for cover and, in so doing, tying the line neatly around an underwater obstruction.

Free-lining a floating bait such as crust is another favoured method. Chub have capacious mouths but choose your bait and hook to match the average size of the fish you can reasonably expect to catch. There is an old and, in many ways, true saying, 'big baits for big fish', but overlarge baits will seldom tempt smaller fish while small bait will frequently lure the largest of specimens. Smear the line with floatant and, when cast, watch the bait carefully as it goes downstream. Chub can take amid a great swirl, or so carefully that the bait just disappears. Watch very intently and, if there is a take, give the fish a moment of two and then strike. Chub frequently lie under overhanging bushes, so try floating a bait into such a spot. A bait can be cast upstream and fished in the reverse way, but make sure the line is gathered to match the speed of the current. If you draw it in at a faster rate the bait will almost certainly be ignored.

Dapping for chub is an ideal method where banks are difficult to fish, or where a narrow stream leaves pockets of deeper water inhabited by solitary fish. Baits for this style of angling should include insects which could fall into the water in a perfectly natural way.

Sunken baits can be presented on orthodox leger rigs – rolling, or static, using a coffin, link or Capta lead – or free-lined either up or downstream. When free-lining sunken baits such as a lob worm or several brandlings, remember that it is vitally important to keep in touch with the bait at all times. This is not a simple style of angling, but it can be a rewarding one, particularly after a flood, when the stream is carrying a lot of additional food which fish such as chub are looking for.

Orthodox legering accounts for many good bags of chub, and the particular style may be chosen to suit a given situation or the chub's changing feeding pattern. The simplest arrangement – a hook tied direct to the reel line, with a lead and a valve rubber stop – can be worked slowly down a stretch of river bed and then left lying in slack water at the tail-end of a run. Upstream legering, as used for barbel fishing, is also a well tried style. When the fish are being particularly shy, a link leger with just a couple of swan shot as weights can be a delicate way of presenting a bait. A paste made from a soft processed cheese is an excellent hook bait when legering.

Although quiver tips are extremely effective with orthodox leger rigs, when free-lining sunken baits or fishing a rolling leger the line should be held so that bites can be felt immediately. Hold the line in a 'V' drawn down between the reel and the bottom ring. When fishing a static leger in fast water, and particularly where both big chub and barbel are caught, it can be an advantage to dispense with the quiver tip and rely on the rod tip, with a 'snubber' fitted about 3 to 4ft up from the weight.

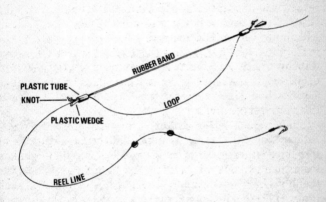

Snubber fitted to line above hook and weights.

When there is a combination of a strong current and a large fish, there can be considerable strain, particularly so if the fish immediately tries to run downstream. This sudden shock loading of a 3 or 4lb BS line can be sufficient to snap it, but the 'snubber' can absorb much of the initial snatch. You then not only save your tackle, but the fish is more likely to be caught.

Chub will take virtually any of the recognised coarse fish baits, plus some which are seldom considered: bread in all its forms, all the accepted worm, maggot and similar baits, luncheon meat, cheese, tripe and bacon rind. Several of the largest chub I have ever caught have taken sand eel fished on a long trail or trace fixed a foot or so up from the weight on a paternoster rig.

Chub are a fascinating species and if you can catch them then your angling skill is equal to any challenge that freshwater fish can offer.

Groundbait

This can be fed into the swim via a swimfeeder/leger, a bait dropper, or as pellets of damp groundbait mixture. As before, do not forget to add samples of the hook bait.

DACE
Leuciscus leuciscus

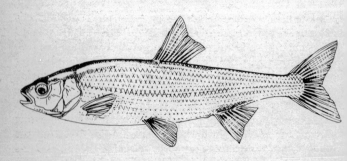

Scale count: LL 48–51. Dorsal and anal fins with concave free edges. British record 1lb 4oz 4dr (574gm).

Distribution and habits

A widely distributed river fish which, although not growing to any great size, is a great favourite with many coarse anglers. Dace will tolerate the conditions provided by quite muddy and slow-flowing rivers, but they thrive better in well aerated, clear water streams offering an abundance of weed growth.

146

They are a lively species which move around in shoals, feeding on insect larvae and various creatures they find amongst the weeds and floating on the surface. Dace are quite tolerant of temperature changes, but during very hot weather they always seek areas offering the most lively water conditions.

Tackle, methods and bait

Successful dace fishing means using light tackle together with a delicate angling approach. Use a long, tip-actioned float rod with line not exceeding 2lb BS. Hook sizes should be 16 to 20, and floats light and sensitive.

As dace will feed at all levels from the bed to the surface, the angler must search the swim to find the fish. Arrange the shot and float carefully so the depth at which the bait is being presented can be regulated as necessary. Take note of both wind and current and adjust the float tackle accordingly.

Float fishing baits include maggots, casters, cooked seeds and grains, bread paste, flake and cube, silkweed and various items such as caddis grubs. Although dace will feed during the brightest part of a summer day, dusk and semi-light of early morning will usually produce the best catches. During the winter months they can be taken on very light leger tackle fished in deeper water.

If the current permits, tie a 16 hook direct to the reel line and use no more than one swan shot about 6in from the hook. Let the current take the bait (possibly the tail-end of a lob worm, or a brandling) into an eddy or stretch of slack water. Both dace and roach could be congregated in such an area. Fly fishing tactics will also catch dace, and occasionally a really large specimen can be lured by a surface-fished bait such as a blow-fly.

Groundbait

Little and often is the best guide, and remember how important it is to get the groundbait going down the swim at a depth similar to that of the hook bait. If the feed is floating on the surface it will either miss the shoal or entice the fish further downstream.

Anquilla anquilla

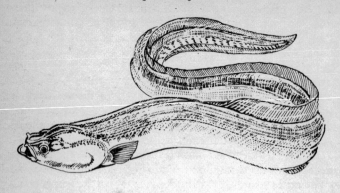

Minute scales embedded in the skin. British record 11lb 2oz (5K 46gm).

Distribution and habits
Most streams, ponds, rivers and lakes have a population of eels. They feed on a wide range of insect larvae, fish spawn and small fish. They are mainly nocturnal creatures which find their food by smell. Eels lie dormant throughout the colder months, but they are particularly active during hot stormy weather in summer.

Tackle, methods and bait
Very few anglers fish specifically for eels, despite the fact that they are both excellent to eat and game fighters. Their bodies are covered in a glutinous yellowish mucous which coats everything it touches and makes them generally unpopular. Those who do fish for them would use a standard leger or bottom fishing rod with a 5 to 8lb BS line if really large fish are expected. Eels can fight like tigers and, pound for pound, few fish fight harder. Fish on the bottom with baits such as worm, dead fish and strips of kipper.

148

Thymallus thymallus

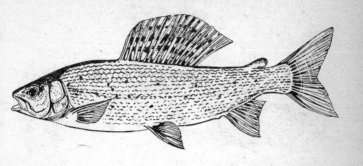

High dorsal fin. 17–24 rays. Adipose fin present. Unmistakable profile. British record 2lb 10¼oz, (1K 197gm).

Distribution and habits
Although found in many parts of the country, they are normally only in those rivers and streams which are suited to trout, a species to which they are related (note the adipose fin). Since they are spring spawners, however, they are classified as coarse fish. They favour streamy runs close to weed beds and they will rise to feed on items carried on the surface, as well as at all levels, in much the same way as dace.

Tackle, methods and baits
Employ standard float tackle and tactics, but keep the tackle light, as for dace fishing. Trot the stream at varying depths until the fish are located and use hooks and baits similar to those used for dace fishing. Light legering tactics can produce good results in winter.

Grayling are an excellent table fish, but never take them unless fishery rules permit.

Groundbait
Adopt the tactics used in dace fishing.

Two dorsal fins. 1. Spiney 14. 2. Spiney 2. Soft 14. Separate fins but joined at base by membrane. Dark vertical stripes on body. Ventral fins. Orange. British record 4lb 12oz (2K 154gm).

Distribution and habits

One of the most widespread of all British coarse fish, perch thrive in both still waters and rivers. Its main requisite is well oxygenated water and it is one of the first species to die as a result of lowering oxygen levels.

Perch are predators and live mainly on smaller fish as well as on various insect larvae and worms. They have a shoaling instinct, and will move around a lake or patrol a section of river actively looking for food. Large perch tend to be more solitary creatures, inhabiting a particular clump of weeds or similar sheltered position during the summer and autumn, but seeking deeper, more sheltered surroundings in very cold weather and floods.

Tackle, methods and bait

Both standard float fishing and light spinning tackle are recommended, and baits include small fish such as minnows as well as both lobworms and brandlings.

Where fishing space is limited, for example between clumps of weed or lily pads, a paternoster rig is useful. In a millpool or downstream of a weir, there are often back eddies and swirls which can be used to carry a float-fished worm or brandlings into various corners and alongside old walls – just the sort of lies chosen by perch.

A minnow or similar small fish used as a bait for the sink and draw method can tempt a really large perch, but spinning is probably the most interesting of all the styles. When spinning for fish such as perch, work to a plan. Never just cast and hope and then cast again in a completely different direction. The diagram here suggests how a spinner can be worked in both running and still water.

By following a set pattern, all the water is covered, and remember to keep changing both the speed and the direction of recovery. Never cast and reel in at a constant speed and in a straight line. Curiously, spinners of a certain type and colour often seem to be more effective on particular waters. Take local advice on this, but generally I have found that dull lures bring the best results on bright days, and vice-versa. Although it is frequently difficult, try to cast from a position which does not frame you against the sky-line. This is not quite so important when either wind or rain is disturbing the surface.

When unhooking your fish, take care to hold it carefully with a cloth. The needle-sharp spines on the dorsal fin can cause ugly wounds.

Groundbait

Light groundbaiting can be used to congregate small fish which in turn may attract either a shoal of perch or one or two large ones.

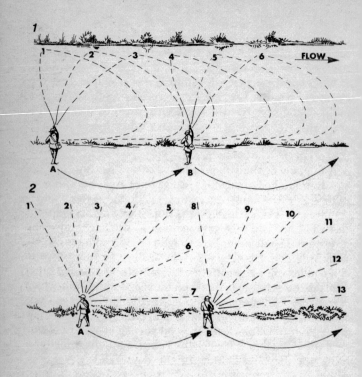

Spinning patterns: 1. River. From position A cast to points 1, 2 and 3. Move to B and cast to points 4, 5 and 6. 2. Lake. By casting at point A from 1 through to 7, the area is well covered. Move to B and cast from 8 through to 13 to cover this area. In both cases when moving from A to B walk well back from the bank and move quietly. Never neglect the strip along the bankside, especially if there is a reeded margin.

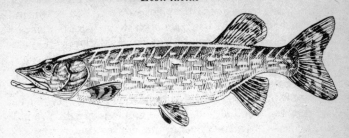

PIKE
Esox lucius

Unmistakable shape. Dorsal and anal fins opposite and close to tail. British record 40lb (18K 143gm).

Distribution and habits

Pike are found in the majority of British waters except for the spate rivers of the far south-west and parts of Wales and Scotland. They are taken from both rivers and lakes, where individual fish normally become established in an area in which they live and feed. Pike lurk amongst reeds and other underwater plants and obstructions, feeding on fish which include smaller ones of their own kind, water fowl, frogs, rats and just about anything edible they can get their massive jaw around. During the coldest weather they tend to become sluggish, but as the water temperature starts to rise after a cold snap, pike fishing can be very exciting.

Tackle, methods and bait

Nothing special is required in the form of tackle, just equipment which is both suited to the style of angling and to the size and power of the fish. Float fish alongside reeds or undercut banks, in fact in any position where it is likely a pike will lie in wait for its prey. For bait, a dead fish such as a sprat can be quite efficient.

When a run develops, do not be in a hurry to strike. Wait for the main float to dive, watch the pilot float and strike sideways, against the run of the fish. Very large pike are frequently more heavy than active and many near 30lb fish have proved to be very disappointing fighters.

Both herring and sprats are excellent baits for leger style fishing. Cast into a deep run or close to a reed bed, set the rod on rests and leave the bale arm open so the fish can make its initial run without feeling restriction. As it moves off after a pause, strike and set the hook. If the fish drops the bait before the hook is set, give it time to come back. Pike will rarely leave a bait once they have found it.

Pike fishing using a legered or floating bait is very much a waiting game and although these methods usually produce the biggest fish, many prefer to spin or use various lures. The latter styles tend to bring a greater number of smaller fish but a 10lb pike on a light-to-medium rod offers a great sporting challenge. Fish the lure deep and slowly. Remember that pike do not chase their prey like perch. They normally make a quick lunge and if the intended victim escapes, they turn away and look for another, easier chance. Pike will not waste time and energy chasing a minnow if they can snap up a 1lb roach without effort.

When spinning or plug fishing, work to a plan similar to the one used when spinning for perch. Never be in a hurry to lift the lure from the water. A pike lying in the reeds close to the spot from which you are casting will frequently show at the very last moment. When a pike hits an artificial lure, strike immediately. Do not give the fish time to reject the metal or plastic object that has fooled it.

Waters that have a lot of bottom weed can be fished with a floating plug, one set to dive as it is reeled in. Operate this in short jerks – a few turns on the reel handle – and then let the plug flutter back to the surface. Because summer weed growth can cost a lot of lures, this style of angling is generally accepted as a winter pastime, but it can be employed at any time if care is taken, and thought is given to choosing the right type of lure. When pike fishing I always use a short wire trace to the hook as these fish have teeth which are quite capable of slicing through nylon. The sink and draw method is also quite effective but, in my experience, it has never produced more or bigger fish than either lure fishing or legering.

Live baiting is now archaic and I find it nowhere near as effective as fishing a dead bait on either float or leger tackle. In fact, even the use of dead freshwater fish is very much a case of choosing second best. I have never found a fish bait which is superior to sprat, herring or mackerel.

Many stories about the dangers of handling pike have been told, and while some are bordering on fantasy, there is no doubt that these fish can be dangerous. However, if you treat them with respect and use the right tools, then the job is relatively simple. Never take a large pike out of the water until it has been played out. It is then much easier to both net and hold. Wrap the fish in a damp cloth and hold it firmly with your hand across its back, just to the rear of its gills. If the fish is very large then also hold the body down by the 'wrist'. At this point it is necessary to have assistance. Unclip the trace from the reel line, slip a suitable gag into its mouth, and then free the hook(s) with a pair of pliers or forceps. Never put your hand into the mouth. The teeth are sharp and the wound they cause will almost certainly turn sceptic unless you have professional attention.

PIKE–PERCH (Zander)
Stizostedion lucioperca

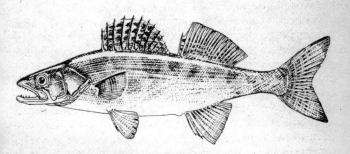

Scale count: LL 80–95. Two dorsal fins, the first spiney, the second spiney 12–14 soft. These fins are separated by a small space. British record 17lb 4oz (7K 824gm).

Similar to Zander, with olive-green back and prominent white spots on second dorsal and tail. LL 80–89. British record 11lb 12oz (5K 329gm).

Distribution and habits

Pike-perch include the walleye and the zander. These fish have a very limited distribution, and most fishery authorities wish to maintain this situation. They are a species which will thrive in both lakes and rivers where they feed on other fish as well as various insects and small creatures.

Tackle, methods and bait

Both zander and walleye will take legered dead fish and worm, as well as spinners.

ROACH
Rutilus rutilus

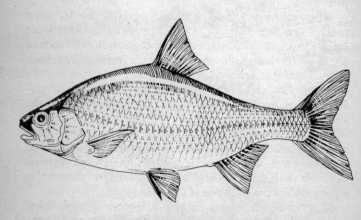

Scale count: LL 42–45. Dorsal fin 9–10 rays, originating above the base of the pelvic fins. British record 4lb 1oz (1K 842gm).

Distribution and habits

This species is found in both still and running water from lowland Scotland to southern England. Roach feed on a variety of insect larvae and similar small creatures as well as vegetable matter. Although they are a shoaling species, the larger specimens seem to be more solitary fish – at least, that has been my experience in the more heavily fished waters. However, where coarse angling pressure is light, for example in parts of Scotland, roach between 1lb and 1½lb can be taken fairly regularly. They always feed most freely at dawn and dusk.

Tackle, methods and bait

Use similar tackle and tactics as for dace fishing, except that legering or laying-on will often lure the larger fish. Choose an area where the current is slack, close to a bed of weeds or lily, and feed very lightly. Big roach will often lay just out of the main current, for example on the edge of a back eddy in a mill pool.

When the stream is carrying a lot of extra colour, white baits such as bread flake or a single maggot on an 18 hook can bring results. Remember, however, that roach tend to feed either on the bottom, or generally lower in the stream than dace. During flood conditions keep the bait close to the sedges and fish deep in those sections out of the main current. In the main, fish have no liking for 'dirty water' because the sediment clogs their gills. They will therefore seek an area where there is least current, and where they can stay as quiet as possible. Activity means greater use of gills as the fish need more oxygen. Canal and still-water angling in general demands the lightest possible tackle. Fishing 'on the drop' is a good style, as is laying-on.

Baits for roach fishing include maggots, casters, flake, cube, paste, caddis grubs, various cooked grains and seeds. These fish can take a bait extremely stealthily. Never ignore a float movement, even if it is only a sideways knock.

Groundbait

Adopt the golden rule, 'little and often', but do not lay a carpet of white crumb or rusk in shallow, clear water and then expect a roach, or any other fish, to cross it. Their natural caution will keep them well away from such an unaccustomed sight.

RUDD
Scardinius erythrophthalmus

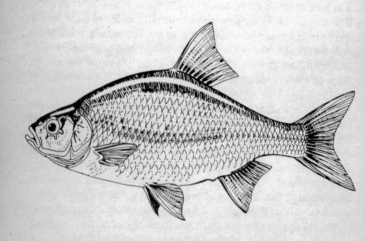

Scale count: LL 40–45. Dorsal fin originates well behind the base of the pelvic fins. 8–9 rays. British record 4lb 8oz (2K 41gm).

Distribution and habits

These fish are found mainly in areas where wet pits, lakes, canals and sluggish streams provide a suitable environment. They like plenty of weed cover, and generally feed on insect larvae, fly and various forms of life they find on the surface and amongst the weed. They are an interesting fish to catch, offering something of a challenge as they can be caught in a variety of ways. Rudd are quite susceptible to falling temperatures and are often dormant during frosty periods.

Tackle, methods and bait

Use light tackle similar to that for dace and roach. Mainly float fishing styles are best, such as 'on the drop', laying-on or, in slow-flowing rivers, trotting the stream close to weed beds or alongside the sedges. Keep the floats as light and as sensitive as possible as rudd are not the boldest of creatures. Use small hooks with baits to match: casters, maggot, small worms, bread flake and paste. Occasionally, particularly during the late summer, I have caught rudd by fishing on the surface. In fact some of the largest rudd I have ever caught – around $2\frac{1}{2}$lb – have been taken this way. Treat the line, right up to the hook, with a floatant, and bait a small hook (a 14, 16 or 18) with a floating caster, a small piece of crust or a blow-fly or similar creature.

Groundbait

Use the occasional pellet of 'cloud' bait, just sufficient to draw the fish. If the rudd are feeding on insects on the surface, a few floating casters may be an encouragement. This can be particularly useful when trying to entice these fish to take a hook baited with a floating caster or a small piece of crust.

TENCH
Tinca tinca

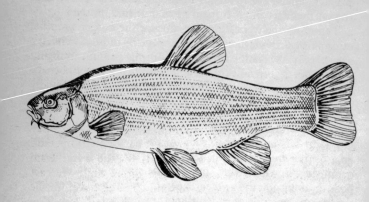

Scales very small, embedded in skin and covered by heavy mucus. In the male fish the second ray of the pelvic fin is swollen. These fins extend beyond the anal vent. British record 10lb 1oz 2dr (4K 567gm).

Distribution and habits

These are a species which favour either rivers which offer well-weeded backwaters and stretches where the stream is sluggish, or lakes, ponds and canals where the same conditions exist. The general area of distribution is similar to that of carp.

Tench are timid creatures which both light and temperature affect quite noticeably. They are similar in many ways to carp, feeding best in a water temperature ranging from about 12°C (55°F) to 21°C (70°F). They also sift the mud and bottom debris for various creatures such as insect larvae and worms. Tench feed on freshwater mussels and snails as well

160

as other small animals they might manage to suck from the vegetation growing along the water's edge. A patch of discoloured water or a line of bubbles on the surface will often pinpoint the whereabouts of feeding tench. As they dredge the bottom they disturb the mud and release gasses.

Tench normally lie dormant during the colder months, particularly in still water. Rivers, especially those which have a generally steadier temperature during the autumn and winter, seem to produce a few tench during late February and March. But the best of the sport with these fish is usually from the opening of the season until the first of the autumn frosts.

Light also seems to be an important factor. Although tench will feed throughout daylight hours, I have noted time and time again that as soon as the sun strikes the water I am fishing, sport gets slower and slower. Either dull, overcast days, or the evening and early morning periods have, for me at least, been the most productive.

Tackle, methods and bait

The average angler can fish for tench perfectly adequately with a standard bottom rod giving a nice through action, a 4 to 5lb BS line, plus the usual assortment of floats, hooks and lead shot. (A fast tip action rod is not suited to this type of angling as tench are a powerful species.) Legering is also a matter of using standard equipment, but keep the line strength up to 5lb BS if casting a swimfeeder. The extra strength is needed to counteract the strain created by the added weight.

For both float and leger tactics, the angler should use line which gives a safety margin. Tench and heavy weed growth are synonymous, and often the fish require a little bullying to keep them away from snags. Never adopt a dogmatic approach to the subject – if conditions suggest using a stronger line, then use one. There are many waters which I fish with a 7lb BS line. I see no point in using tackle which gives me very little chance of being able to play the fish correctly, land and then remove the hook and set the creature free.

Much has been said and written about preparing the swim. Raking the bed is one popular scheme. The disturbed area attracts tench, particularly if it is also fairly liberally carpeted with an acceptable ground bait. Unfortunately, the average angler has to accept conditions as they are, not as he would like them to be. The majority of club waters have a series of well ordered swims and anyone who suddenly cut a swath through a bed of reeds would meet severe disapproval from the committee. There would also be considerable comment from those fishing nearby swims if, on arrival, the newcomer immediately threw a rake-like drag into the water and began disrupting a wide area. If circumstances allow, by all means rake the area, providing it is a reasonably clean bed. If by dragging you are only disturbing the muck of ages, releasing clouds of evil smelling gases and generally poisoning that section of the lake, then do not bother. The result will almost certainly be an exodus of all the fish.

To a very great extent, the actual method of fishing will be decided by the conditions, and on large waters this often means legering. This can be the only method by which you can place your bait in the area you consider most likely to hold fish. In trying to decide where the fish are likely to be, one would not go far wrong by assuming that tench feed in much the same areas as those chosen by carp. For example, a lake with a bed shelving from the edge to a depth of, say, 10ft at a distance of 25 to 35ft out, might well have a fair amount of weed growing on the bottom. Expect to find tench feeding amongst the weed growth in deep water during the day, but coming very close to the edge at dusk and in the pre-dawn twilight.

When it is possible to use a float fishing technique, adopt the lift method, a style which has brought me some very good catches. This is not the easiest of ways when conditions are against you. A stiff breeze breaking the surface is just one of the various problems the float angler faces, and so a leger rig must often be considered. A swimfeeder/leger is useful, but on a hard-fished water it may well be that the splash made by this rig would prove disturbing to the fish you hope to catch. It is possible that better results could be obtained by employing a link leger with just two or three swan shot.

When fishing an area where the bed has a heavy coating of weed, a semi-buoyant leger weight can help to overcome the problems which arise when the lead sinks into the weed, carrying the line with it. Fashion a piece of balsa wood into a 2in-long cigar-shaped plug, drill lengthways and insert a piece of thin polythene tubing (the ink reservoir from a ball-point pen would do). Fix the tube with a suitable adhesive. Cut a groove around the plug and into this hollow lay sufficient lead wire to make the balsa wood plug sink very slowly. A leger weight of this type will lay on top of the weed blanket, and greatly facilitate quick striking.

A bomb-shaped lead attached to a link can also be used to fish over a weed bed, but often the lead will tangle with the plants. The angler can then be faced by the problems of a lively fish hooked onto a line which is running through a nylon loop which in turn is fixed to a lead that is well and truly snagged by weed. At this point we come back to my earlier remarks about using a line which gives a safety margin.

Bite detectors for leger-style fishing are similar to those used when carp fishing. I have rarely found it necessary to use anything more complicated than a pellet of dough squeezed onto the line, either at the bottom of a loop drawn down between the reel and first ring, or a foot or so down from the top ring.

Occasionally, tench can be caught on free-lined and surface-fished baits. When free-lining, set up your rod on two rests and watch the line carefully. Fix your attention on the spot where it enters the water and strike as the line moves. It sometimes helps if a small piece of dough is squeezed onto the line between the reel and first or butt ring. This method demands the utmost concentration, but it can be successful on hard-fished waters where the fish are hook-shy.

The 'floating crust' technique is also a tench catcher and some will suggest using this style where the surface of the water is largely covered with lily pads. The system works, but tackle capable of instant control is necessary for very obvious reasons. However, deliberately choosing conditions which demand such tactics is not for me.

Tench baits are, in the main, similar to those used for carp fishing and include the use of a variety of flavourings in paste. When fishing over weed, do not ignore balanced crust. This can be most effective, but remember that tench are a much smaller species than carp, so baits should be scaled down to match. Maggots are an excellent bait, especially if used in conjunction with bread flake squeezed around the hook shank.

Groundbait

Generally as for carp, but the additional placing of 'cloud' bait can increase interest. This can be made by encasing dry cloud bait with a dryish mixture of ordinary groundbait. As the ball hits the water the casing should disintegrate and sink quite rapidly. The dry bait is then freed to disperse and 'cloud' or colour the water as desired.

In still water, a swimfeeder can be used to distribute cloud bait. Pack the centre with the dry powder (I sometimes use a mixture of equal parts of cornflour and custard powder, plus a few samples of hook bait), seal both ends of the feeder with a dryish mixture of groundbait, and then cast into the target area. Give the swimfeeder time to reach the bottom, reel in slowly until the weight of the feeder can be felt and then give a sharp jerk or two on the line. This should release the cloud bait in just the right place. Groundbait can also be pressed around the weights on a link leger, but this method does not stand up to vigorous casting.

Finally, do not forget the importance of including samples of hook bait with the ground feed. This is probably the most important aspect of all the many facets of groundbaiting.

TROUT (Brown)
Salmo trutta fario

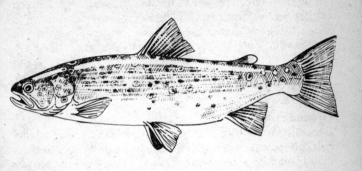

Tail fin square cut. Numerous black spots extending below lateral line often with lighter halo. Also numerous red spots. Adipose fin has orange edge. British record 19lb 9oz 4dr (8K 880gm).

Distribution and habits
This species requires a special environment if it is to thrive. The water must be oxygen-rich and relatively cool, and hold a good supply of small animals and insect larvae. There must also be suitable areas of gravel in which the females can lay their eggs in the late autumn to winter.

Tackle, methods and bait
Fly and spinning techniques are invariably the rule, but in some areas worm baits are permitted. It is usually accepted that the majority of trout waters are strictly controlled. These are managed either by bodies such as Regional Water Authorities, landowners, hotels and clubs or by syndicates of one kind or another. Always look for, and take, whatever local advice there is available about both tackle and methods, as something accepted on one river or lake may not be permitted on a water close by.

TROUT (Rainbow)
Salmo gairdneri

Tailfin slightly concave. Distinct iridescent strip along side. Dense black spotting on the back, dorsal, adipose and tail fins. British record 19lb 8oz (8K 844gm).

Distribution and habits
These fish are widely distributed as a result of the stocking policies adopted by water authorities. Most 'put and take' reservoirs and lake fisheries, as well as some rivers, are fed with a regular supply of rainbows. Reared in hatcheries, they seldom breed to any appreciable extent in British waters. The original stock was imported into the UK from North America at around the turn of the century. Their habits are in line with those of brown trout in that they feed on small animals and insect larvae and will respond to similar angling techniques.

Tackle, methods and bait
The remarks on tackle and methods for brown trout apply equally to rainbows. There is, however, one important fact about tackle which must be remembered when considering

reservoir fishing, particularly if the water is large and open. These big expanses of water can be very windswept areas, and this calls for heavier lines and more powerful rods. Without the additional weight, possibly an 8 or 9 line, it can be impossible to cast the required distance.

It is also essential to keep going along the bank, casting and moving a step or so at a time until a fish is found. Cast to a pattern, never just throw a line indiscriminately. This, of course, depends entirely on the number of anglers there are, as crowded banks would make such moves very unpopular. In any event, try to offer your fly or nymph to as many fish as possible, rather than relying on them coming to you.

It takes quite a time to get to know a water, but by fishing to a pattern and recording both your successes and failures, you will soon acquire the knowledge and skill necessary to master the subject. There are occasions, such as during a drought, or through building or maintenance work, that the level of the reservoir may be extremely low. Take this opportunity to make a few sketches of the bed. Note the line of old hedgerows and ditches, or similar areas where, when the reservoir is full, trout might well lie.

Remember, too, that wind-ruffled water not only reduces the trout's ability to see you, but it also makes it more difficult for predators to spot the fish. In these conditions, they will often feed in relatively shallow water, particularly on the downwind side of a lake, so don't neglect areas you can cover easily.

Beginners can get into quite a tangle when retrieving line. Some even wind the slack around their fingers, and eventually they get into a fine old muddle. Keep it simple: either learn to gather the line in a figure of eight, holding the line in the palm of one hand and the rod in the other; or pull the line in with one hand while holding the rod in the other, with the line running between the forefinger and rod so that it can be held firmly while the line-gathering hand is moving up ready to repeat the pulling action.

If you are wading, a floating line can be dropped onto the water; if fishing from the bank, use a line tray. It is, however, most useful to learn the knack of picking up the line in a figure of eight. This makes for much easier casting. A few moments tuition from a bailiff or fellow angler is all that is needed to learn this quite simple, yet highly effective method.

When fishing a nymph, never be in a hurry. Cast and let it settle for a moment or two before starting to retrieve. Occasionally – and here again it depends on both wind direction and the amount of clear bank space – it is possible to cast and then let the wind carry the nymph slowly over the bottom as you walk along the bank. The wind blowing on the line will be sufficient to move the nymph, but take care to walk at a speed equal to the drift. Sometimes a floating buzzer can be fished in a similar way.

Always take local advice about particular patterns of flies and other fine details. Bailifs and wardens are a mine of valuable information. They will respect you all the more for having the good sense to seek their skilled advice.

SEA TROUT
Salmo trutta

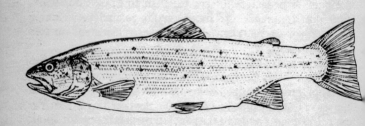

Upper jawbone extends beyond the level of eyes; 14 major rays on dorsal fin; tailfin more square cut than salmon, black spots on sides extending below lateral line. The British record is open at the time of writing but claims for fish of 15lb (6K 804gm) would be considered.

168

Distribution and habits

Sea trout are found in many rivers in the British Isles and, in common with other members of their family, they require special conditions for both spawning and for their young to thrive. They have a life-cycle similar to salmon, with the young migrating seawards and returning to spawn after a span of a year or so. Their migratory tendency is not generally as pronounced as the salmons', and the mortality rate following spawning is not as high. Sea trout are, like salmon, an extremely valuable asset, so any worthwhile fishing is always well controlled. And although it is not so highly priced as salmon, sea trout fishing is still relatively expensive to obtain. Sea trout rivers, in common with those holding salmon, have runs which peak at different times of the year. The best runs usually occur during July and August.

Tackle, methods and bait

Most successful sea trout anglers tend to devote their time and energy learning all they can about the particular waters they fish. Inevitably, this leads to highly individual choices of tackle to suit the many differing conditions in sea trout rivers. Local advice is absolutely essential when it comes to detailed selection of tackle but, broadly speaking, a 9ft fly rod matched with an 8 or 9 weight line should prove adequate. For spinning, choose a rod designed to cast a lure weighing around 1½oz (about 40gm), and this means using an 8 to 10lb BS line.

The curious thing about angling for sea trout is the fact that night fishing, particularly during the first couple of hours of darkness, is generally the most productive period of the day. Obviously, they are taken at other times, but my experience has always been that activity is greatest for about two hours after dusk. During this period use a floating line and a locally recommended fly. I have found a wet fly, such as a teal blue and silver, is very effective if fished close to the surface, working it in the current and drawing it back across before recovering and re-casting.

Never ignore the ripply broken water at the tail-end of a pool. Often you will find that fish seem to take more readily in one part of a pool than another. As the night progresses, you may well find that by changing your technique and fishing deep with a sinking line another sea trout or two might be tempted. At the first hint of the approach of dawn, change once again to presenting your fly either close to, or on the surface.

Fishing at night creates a number of problems, the most important of which is safety. I would not recommend lone expeditions, particularly on unfamiliar territory. Never fish a water for the first time at night, and never enter a stream without either an intimate knowledge of the bed and whatever hazards there may be, and carrying and using a wading staff or stick. Other points which should be noted about night fishing include the possibility of a sudden and alarming rise in the water level following a storm miles away. Many sea trout and salmon rivers are capable of rising a couple of feet or so in the time it takes to wade perhaps no more than 30 paces to the point of exit. Alone, and at night, this can indeed be a frightening experience. There is also the possibility that earlier floods have scoured out deep holes where previously there were banks of shingle, and the sudden collapse of an undercut bank can also have disastrous consequences. The dangers of falling into deep water at night and alone are obvious.

When fishing in the dark, I always establish a 'base' marked by a small oil lamp. This glimmer not only provides a useful reference point, but it also serves as a guide to the easiest point of exit from the water. This can be invaluable if you have just caught a 10lb fish.

Frequently, especially when spawned fish (kelts) are coming downstream, gaffs are prohibited. This means using either a net or a 'tailer' – a flexible steel rod with a handle at one end and a plaited loop at the other. The loop is slipped over the fish's tail and pulled tight and the fish can then be lifted from the water and carried to the bank. Dispatch the fish immediately with a hard blow on the head with a priest (having first made sure that it is not a 'kelt' or spent fish).

Tailing can also be done by hand, but play the fish right out before attempting it, and then make sure that you do it swiftly and firmly. As you draw the fish in, it will be lying head into the stream, so when fishing from the right bank, hold the rod in the left hand and tail with the right. Change hands for the opposite bank. The left bank is on left hand side when looking downstream, the right bank on the right. Tailing by hand is not as difficult as it may sound. Grasp the wrist (the narrow section adjoining the caudal or tail fin) with the thumb and forefinger encircling the wrist and close to the tail. When using a tailer adopt a similar procedure, in other words when fishing from the right bank hold the rod in the left hand and use the tailer with the right.

Always hold the fish away from your body, particularly when tailing by hand. If the fish gives a sudden and violent twist, it can knock itself free by banging against your leg. My previous remarks about knowing the water and not fishing an unfamiliar stream at night would be brought home very forcibly if, as often happens with sea trout, the first one you hooked took off like a train and rushed downstream into a territory you did not know. When this occurs, I always let the fish take line while checking the outflow only very lightly. As soon as its first run slows, I tighten up. From then on, make the fish fight for every inch of line it takes.

Never be in a hurry to either strike or recover line. Sea trout are strong creatures, and bullying them often results in a snapped leader. Try to avoid what might be called a 'slash strike'. It really isn't necessary. When fishing a wet fly you need do no more than 'tighten' or 'firm-up' the line by drawing in whatever slack there may be and lifting the rod so that it is in the correct attitude to absorb strain. An exaggerated sweeping strike can easily either snap the leader if the fish is 'running' or possibly pull the fly straight out of its mouth.

Sometimes during daytime fishing you will see the fish stopping short of the fly, not once, but time after time. These fish are called 'short risers'. All you can do is either keep offering the fly in the hope that you will eventually tease the fish into making a fatal mistake, or change the fly, either increasing or decreasing its size.

When hooked, both sea trout and salmon sometimes have

a habit of going to the bottom or taking refuge behind a large stone or rock, and then sulking or refusing to move. Obviously, a really large fish in such a situation can take some shifting, particularly so if it's in an inaccessible spot. You might try a few well-aimed stones, or you could change your position and try the slack line technique or a sharp tug.

Daytime river fishing for sea trout has, for me at least, only been successful when I have used either a small wet or dry fly. Nymph fishing can also be successful and once or twice, when conditions have been favourable, dapping has brought a fish or two.

In some parts of Scotland, being taken out onto a sea loch by an experienced gillie can provide some memorable sport. When considering either sea trout or salmon fishing, always remember the importance of the time of year and the state of the water. Never embark on a sea trout or salmon fishing expedition unless you either possess the necessary local knowledge or you have taken steps to equip yourself with it.

SALMON
Salmo salar

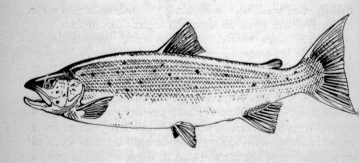

Caudal peduncle narrow. Tailfin is shallowly forked. Upper and lower rays show as 'horns'. British record 64lb (29K 29gm).

172

Distribution and habits

All the remarks about sea trout apply generally to salmon, except that salmon are less widely distributed and are not found in many rivers with a good run of migratory trout. Fishing for salmon is normally a considerably more expensive pastime and even rod licence charges are sometimes higher. Both rod licences and permits are normally the most expensive of all.

Tackle, methods and bait

Use fly rods and lines similar to those described for sea trout fishing. In some areas, however, both conditions and the size of the fish would make stronger tackle advisable. For example, you might use a rod about 15ft long and a 10 or 11 weight line, while for spinning rods, you could use a 10ft rod constructed to cast 2oz (approx. 55gm) lines.

Assume that all salmon rivers are strictly controlled and the fishing rights held by a landowner, hotel, private syndicate or some kind of association.

It is not a sport which one just 'does'. There must be prior organisation, including arrangements to gain access to a fishable stretch of river. Although a reasonably competent fly or spin fisher would be able to angle successfully for salmon, local conditions must be considered. Once again we return to the oft given advice – seek local opinion about baits, times to fish and tackle details. In no branch of fishing is this more important than when undertaking angling for salmon.

In many ways, fly fishing for salmon is very similar to angling for sea trout, except that salmon are more likely to leap, and when first hooked they often tend to be more violent. If the fish does break water, lower the rod tip immediately so that it cannot throw its weight against a line which is under strain. Never hold a newly hooked fish on a tight line as the creature will most probably hesitate for a moment or two at first and then shake itself strenuously in an attempt to shed the hook. After making an initial run, a salmon will often double back, leaving the unprepared fisher with a mass of slack line. Always maintain contact with the fish, and although only light pressure is advisable at the start,

173

ensure that the fish strains for every inch of line it takes. By making it fight continually against the spring in the rod, you will eventually weaken the creature sufficiently to either gaff or, preferably, tail it.

As baits and methods are normally the subject of fishery rules, always pay great attention to whatever restrictions exist.

Briefly, my advice to anyone going salmon fishing for the first time would be to go to a water where the skilled advice of a gillie was available. Spend as much time with him as possible, and if you absorb enough to realise that there is still a lifetime of learning ahead, then you are partway towards becoming a successful angler.

Sea angling

When considering the various methods used to catch sea fish, it soon becomes apparent that in many instances conditions, rather than the species of fish being sought, influence the choice of tackle to a very large extent. For example, the mechanics of casting from the beach means using a rod some 10 to 12ft long. Tidal and weather conditions can dictate both the weight and the style of lead. Vigorous casting places an enormous strain on the line, so a stronger one is required when using a 6oz lead as against another of half that weight.

Similar remarks can be made about boat fishing equipment, especially for ground or bottom fishing in deep water in areas where tidal currents are strong. There are times and places where a 1lb lead weight (or even more) is necessary to hold the tackle in position. This fact alone dictates the use of a very powerful rod and strong line, possibly totally out of proportion to the size and power of the fish the angler can reasonably expect to catch. The same species can be caught in different places using a variety of techniques, but here again it is the situation in which the angler is placed which so often determines the method he will use.

Sea angling therefore tends to become structured into shore, rock, inshore/shallow water boat fishing and deep water angling. Each has its own series of variations on what is, after all, a common theme of basic tackle arrangements. It is these variations which catch fish.

Beach fishing

Throughout the course of the year different species become available to the beach angler. There is no set overall pattern to this change which varies from area to area. For example, along parts of the southern and south-eastern coastline, the spring may bring sport with plaice and flounders, with bass and eels starting to put in an appearance during May. These species might be joined by mullet and bream in June, and from time to time other fish such as mackerel, garfish and dabs might well be caught.

The autumn brings about a change. Summer visitors such as mackerel and garfish leave, and though flounder and bass are still around, silver whiting and codling can arrive. During the colder months, the catches mainly consist of flounders, whiting, codling, plus an assortment of other lesser species such as pouting and rockling.

Eventually, possibly January or February, flounder go out into deeper water for spawning, returning perhaps during late March or April, and so the year begins once again. Elsewhere there is also a changing pattern, but the species may be different.

Local conditions set the pattern to a large extent over which basic tackle anglers in the area need. There are, however, a number of refinements to both tackle and techniques which can help quite considerably.

All tackle is expensive and so it should be well maintained. If it is not, efficiency is impaired to a quite amazing extent. General conditions on the foreshore are extremely tough on both rod and reel, and the line also takes a vast amount of wear. Take particular note of the state of all the rod rings. Any with sharp edges, grooves and rough spots must be replaced, as they will rapidly ruin your line. Pay attention to the joints and keep them clean. They should fit firmly and easily.

The reel is extremely vulnerable. Only fish with one designed for use in a marine environment, and always pay

1. Bass, Dicentrachus labrax, 18lb 2oz 8K 220gm. 2. Cod,
Gadus morhua, 44lb 8oz 20K 183gm. 3. Dab, Limanda
limanda, 2lb 9oz 8dr 1K 176gm. 4. Flounder, Platichthys flesus,
5lb 2oz 2K 324gm. 5. Mullet, Chelon labrosus, 14lb 2oz 12dr
6K 427gm. 6. Plaice, Pleuronectes platessa, 8lb 1oz 4dr 3K
664gm. 7. Sole, Solea solea, 4lb 8oz 2K 41gm. 8. Whiting,
Merlangius merlangus, 3lb 7oz 6dr 1K 569gm. All the weights
refer to shore-caught records. There is a separate list for boat-
caught fish.

particular attention to cleaning and oiling. Some anglers have the wrong idea about lubricants and use heavier ones than those recommended, believing that a heavy oil or even grease can give greater protection. Apart from acting like a breaking agent, the addition of a small amount of sand or grit will turn the grease into little more than a grinding paste from which the reel bearing will suffer. For maximum performance, keep the reel spotlessly clean and only use the lubricant recommended by the manufacturer.

Line takes a vast amount of punishment, both from the shock loading which occurs every cast, and also while lying on the sea bed. Casting is particularly damaging because the wear takes place at roughly the same spot time after time. Overcome this problem by using a leader of a much greater breaking strain than the main line. This will absorb the extra punishment during casting and also provide the extra strength so often needed when landing a large fish in a raking surf.

One of the quickest ways of blunting a hook is to draw it across the sea bed where it will strike against stones and rub through sand and shingle. Using a blunt hook is also one of the best ways of losing a fish. It doesn't take more than a minute or so to run a stone over the hook point. A really sharp hook not only penetrates the fish's jaw more efficiently, it is also easier to bait. Always carry a selection of leads of different type and weight, so that changing conditions can be countered as quickly as possible.

Although there is a considerable amount of similarity between the basic tackle used by all beach anglers, there is, of course, a great variation in both the way in which the terminal rigs are assembled, and in the types and size of the items of equipment used. The paternoster is probably the most widely used tackle arrangement for beach fishing. Since the weight is at the end, leading the tackle in flight, it tends to prevent the line and hooks becoming entangled. A bomb-shaped weight is, from the purely casting standpoint, the most efficient. A snag-strewn seabed can be fished with, for example, a break-away lead or, as explained earlier, with a weight attached to a 'rotten bottom'. The prongs on a break-away lead fold back when jerked, helping the lead to break clear of its holdfast.

A leger rig is also popular, but I seldom use one when casting to the limit. I prefer to use a leger only when fishing from a point where vigorous casting is unnecessary, such as a pier or a jetty. For although the method has some advantages (for example, the fish can take the bait and draw line without feeling the weight of the lead) I still feel that its tendency to tangle while in flight is a hazard that outweighs any fishing advantage.

Beach anglers are best served in the long run by terminal rigs which are as simple as possible. I do not believe that complicated tackle arrangements catch fish. Success comes from using top-quality bait on a hook matched to its purpose, and fished with thought and great concentration.

Smaller species such as plaice, flounder, dab, sole and whiting can all be caught on thin wire long shank hooks, size 1 or 2, but never be shy of using one slightly smaller if the size of the bait warrants it. This is particularly true when angling for mullet with red ragworm bait. I have taken these fish on both size 6 and 8 freshwater hooks. Thin wire long shank hooks not only accept a worm bait very well, they are also easier to remove from the generally smaller mouths of fish such as plaice, sole, flounder and dab. The shank can be gripped with either pliers or forceps. Soft crab is wonderful bait for both plaice and flounders, as is white ragworm – if you can find it.

Although flounders and whiting are what might be described as a 'standard winter combination' in many areas, it is always wise to consider the possibility of hooking a cod. These are large, carpet-bag mouthed fish, and while codling of 5 to 7lb could be held on a hook suited to flounder or plaice, larger fish demand the use of bigger and stronger hooks, such as forged stainless steel, sizes 3/0 or 4/0. Cod baits include crab, several large lugworm on one hook, strip or a small whole squid, strip or a flank of mackerel or herring and large sand eels, all of which are first class. A mixed bait of lug and slipper limpet is also favoured in areas where limpets are washed up onto the beach by storms.

For general angling purposes, all sea fish can be considered to be predatory. Some are probably more interested in feeding on worms, various molluscs and crustaceans, while others vigorously pursue fish smaller than themselves. Both whiting and cod scoop up vast quantities of smaller fish. Examine the contents of the stomach of a freshly caught whiting, and frequently you will find it crammed with sprat and the young of many species. Whiting is probably a greater eater of other fish than cod. Small herring and sprats figure largely in their diet, as do shrimps and crabs. So never ignore the possibility of using a small whole fish, sprats, for example, as bait. This can present casting problems, but this difficulty can be overcome.

During the winter months, surprisingly large numbers of small pouting are sometimes caught quite close to the shore and both cod and whiting are likely to be attracted by these 'food fish'. Having caught one or two, you will soon learn to identify the 'feel' of a pouting bite. When you have hooked one, leave it where it is, setting your tethered fish as an attractive offering to a much larger whiting or cod. If the ploy works, do not be in a hurry to strike, as initially the hook and bait can be pulled out of your main quarry's mouth.

A small butterfish, often found in pools left by the receding tide, is an excellent bait for both cod and whiting. Remember that whiting often feed at a higher level than cod, because they are often more concerned with hunting small fish while cod are dredging the bottom for crabs, worms and shrimps. Consider the positioning of the top hook and make sure it is presenting the bait two or three feet off the bottom. If others are catching whiting and you are not, this could be the reason.

Much has been said and written in recent years about groundbaiting procedures, but most of these ideas founder on the rock of presentation. To be effective, the source of the groundbait must be adjacent to the hook. If you are casting into an area possibly 140 to 150 yards out where there may be 6 or 8ft of water even at low tide, the problems are obvious.

If tidal circumstances permit – and assuming local bye-laws are not broken – it might be possible to peg out an open-weave sack full of minced fish offal and bran. Fix a float marker to a suitable length of line, and when the tide comes in cast into the target area. Remember the direction of the current and place your hook downstream of the groundbait sack. It may be possible to fix a sack of groundbait to the end of a groyne or marker post, but these are not tactics for use during the swimming season, and of course the sack must always be recovered.

Some anglers attach a small piece of sponge to the trace just above the hook, while others even fix a small container (with a wick-like leader protruding through the stopper) adjacent to the weight. Both the section of sponge and the container hold pilchard or similar fish oil. Even cod-liver oil capsules purchased from a chemist for medicinal use are sometimes pushed up onto the hook shank, but such practices are financially prohibitive.

A rod which is constantly attended and watched for the slightest indication of a bite will produce more fish than a set of tackle decorated with all manner of fancy groundbaiting devices. This does not mean that a fresh dug worm or a fillet cut from a firm-fleshed mackerel or herring will fail to be made even more attractive by a dip in a jar of pilchard oil. Such an addition can prove effective but, for all that, a worm bait drawn slowly over the sea bed will usually be far more attractive to a flounder or plaice than one lying still, even if it has been dipped in fish oil.

When fishing from a pier, it will often be found that a bait cast up-tide and then reeled in very slowly, will catch more flounders than one cast down-tide and just left lying on the bed. Flounders are drawn to movement. The spurts of mud and sand created by the tackle are probably similar to that sent up by a crab burrowing and, to a flounder, that means food!

Weed can be a great problem, and when there's an excess of the stuff, you might just as well pack up. Weed isn't wholly bad, however, particularly when there are thick patches of it on the beach and relatively small amounts actually floating around. Flies lay eggs in the weed, and the maggots are eaten by fish, especially mullet. Weed which has been thrown up beyond the tide line is often full of maggots during the summer. If the local authority clear the beach, or the weed is taken back into the water in a storm, fish will soon come quite close in to scavenge. Try baiting a relatively small hook, only use a light weight and fish close to where the weed is being turned over by the tide. This works in the same way in areas where, for example, slipper limpet has been washed up and has died in the sun. Succeeding tides draw it back for the fish to eat.

Although competent long-distance casting is the general aim and ambition of all beach anglers, it certainly isn't essential on every occasion. In fact, it is as easy to cast beyond the area in which the fish are feeding as it is to be unable to cast far enough.

Long casting is really only one of a number of weapons in the angler's armoury, and many would argue that concentration is as important as any. There is very little point in using excellent bait on a needle-sharp hook, casting accurately and then wandering off, leaving your rod perched up on a rest. Either hold your rod or concentrate your attention as hard as you can on the tip. Be as ready to strike at a bite which relaxes all the tension on your line and rod, as you are to hit a fish which takes the bait and immediately moves out to sea. There is, of course, no reason why it should swim towards deeper water. If the fish is already coming shorewards when it picks up your bait, why shouldn't it continue in roughly the same direction?

Speed is the essence of striking at a fish coming towards you. There is hardly any point in just throwing the rod tip back over your shoulder as you will not pick up sufficient line to make contact. Pick up the rod and move back up the beach, start reeling in and then strike hard. If there is still no contact, keep moving back until there is.

Another species which is frequently caught close to the shore is bass. These fish are great hunters and scavengers and they often look for their food amongst the tumbling breakers sometimes in no more water than it takes to cover their backs. The waves flush sand eels and crabs from the sand and mud, and so these two items rank high as baits. Shrimps, sand hoppers and small fish are eaten by bass, as well as the young of a variety of species. Bass are great opportunists. They seem to have the ability to know where the best pickings are to be found and they often appear to move around in concert with tidal influences. They will frequently (and this particularly applies to estuaries and harbours) move in a discernible pattern, changing position to take advantage of whatever edible debris or small creatures may be brought to them by changing currents. Although considerable local knowledge is obviously a great advantage, bass will sometimes betray their position by driving small fish to the surface and this, in turn, will attract sea birds.

The majority of anglers, however, fish open stretches of beach, from rocks and headlands and in sheltered sandy bays. For most, a large bass is a hoped-for bonus, not a certainty, and in recent years the total stock has declined. Conservation is now the order of the day, so never retain a bass less than 15 inches long.

Soft crab is the best all-round bait when shore fishing. Present it on either leger or paternoster tackle, but remember that bass will, in all probability, be following the advancing tide, so long casting is not always best. I have often caught four and five pounders in water no more than 12 or 18 inches deep, which means that leger tackle using a 2 to 3ft-long trace can be an excellent basic approach. Use either a single or two hook-trace, but if using two hooks put a different bait on each. The bait will be swept around in the tide, and present itself in a most attractive way.

There are occasions when, without the benefit of local knowledge, it is difficult to choose the point from which to fish. A sandy bay locked in by two rocky headlands may appear to offer a better chance if fished from the rocks at either end, but if there are sand eels along the shore, the bass are far more likely to be following the making tide, just waiting to scoop up the eels. In this instance, the central area is more likely to yield fish as the tide comes in.

During the latter stages of the ebb or during slack water at low tide, spinning from the rocks might be your best approach. Of course, this general plan is not always applicable, but I have fished a number of such places where this strategy has produced results.

Night angling, particularly during the period just before dawn, is probably the most productive period of all. Calm summer nights can see bass coming amazingly close in, and on many occasions I have felt them strike my legs while wading and fishing in less than a foot of water. Once again, shore fishing would seem to be most productive as the tide is making.

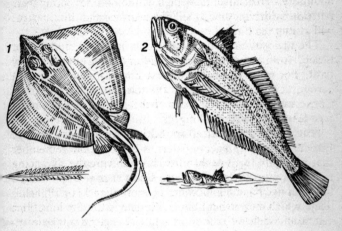

1. Stingray. 2. Weever.

Although bass are usually thought of primarily as a summer and autumn species, quite a number are caught during the winter, so never give up hope entirely, especially in areas where there are special circumstances such as outflow of cooling water from a power station.

Although the specialist bass angler is likely to use a less powerful rod than the general beach angler, most of them fish with perfectly standard equipment – a normal production rod built to cast a 4 to 6oz lead, a reel line of about 20lb BS, plus a leader if necessary. All the earlier remarks about hook sizes apply equally to bass fishing. A size 3/0 or 4/0 would probably match a crab bait, but a smaller hook is more suited to sand eel. Both king rag and lug worm take their share of bass, but whenever possible I would use soft crab.

Never use a rest when fishing deliberately for bass. Hold the rod all the time and concentrate continually. At the first intimation of a bite be prepared to let the fish take some line, lower the rod tip slightly and, as the fish takes off, lift the tip and strike firmly. Be ready to yield line again if the fish is large and very lively.

Never fish at night alone and without the means of providing light. Use either an electric hand lamp or, preferably, a pressure lantern such as a Tilley. For night fishing, an electric lamp fixed to a headband can be extremely useful.

Never wade when breakers are creating a dangerous undertow, and while landing a fish through breakers take care not to be caught by the extra large rogue wave which appears from time to time. Watch the path taken by an oncoming tide and make sure that it doesn't run behind you and cut off your retreat. Certain fish are also dangerous. The weever and the stingray are fairly common, and both can cause serious injury.

There are two weevers, the lesser and greater. Neither are of interest to anglers, but both have venomous spines on the first dorsal fin and gill cover. The lesser weever is an inshore species, and often lies half-submerged in mud or sand. It can be stepped on or picked up while collecting bait or sorting through the contents of a shrimping net. It can also take a bait which can give problems, particularly at night.

Both weevers are similar and have a brownish back with yellowish sides decorated with dark, slanting stripes. The lesser weever may be around 6 inches long, the greater, a deep-water fish, up to 18 inches. If you catch one, pin it down with a piece of wood or even a boot. Cut it clear of the hook and bury it. Do not just discard a weever, as their venom is still active after death. Always seek medical treatment if it stings you.

Stingray are caught by both shore anglers and, more often, boat anglers. They can be large, up to 50 or 60lb. The sting is on the tail, and it takes the form of a particularly nasty jagged-edged spine (sometimes two) which the fish lashes about when caught. The whip-like tail must be pinned down and cut off immediately the fish is landed. Kill the fish with a heavy blow or a knife thrust straight down between the eyes. The spine can inject venom into the wound it causes and, although unlikely, it might be fatal. If injured by a stingray you need medical treatment as soon as possible.

Landing fish when angling from the shore is usually best done with a gaff if the fish is large enough. Mostly they can be drawn clear of the water by the tackle on which they are hooked, and this applies particularly to flounders, plaice and dabs. Never take chances with larger fish such as cod and bass. Mullet are very easy to lose because their lips are surprisingly soft and they are often lost while being landed through the surf. When fishing from a pier or jetty always use a drop-net. Play the fish over it and then lift it clear. Drop-nets are sometimes useful when fishing from rocks, too.

Rock fishing

First and foremost, it must be appreciated that this can be an extremely dangerous pastime. Merely scrambling over rocks to find a suitable position for angling can be hazardous without the added encumberance of rods and a tackle box. Always use recognised paths and remember you are going fishing, not mountaineering.

It is not over-dramatising to say that even on what appears to be the calmest of days, freak swells suddenly sweep over exposed rocks, and every year lives are lost. It is impossible to over-emphasise the dangers which can accompany this style of sea angling. Visitors to an unfamiliar area should always seek advice from HM Coastguards, local fishermen or RNLI personnel. It is not a sign of weakness to ask for advice, but rather an indication that the enquirer knows what he's about and has sufficient experience to recognise problem areas when he sees them.

Apart from being swept away, it is also extremely easy to be cut off by a rising tide. Never fish alone. Even a simple accident such as a sprained or broken ankle can develop into a tragedy if help is not available.

Having taken sensible precautions, there is no reason why

1. Coalfish, *Pollachius virens*, 18lb (8K 164gm). 2. Conger, *Conger conger*, 67lb 1oz (30K 417gm). 3. Ling, *Molva molva*, 15lb 5oz 11dr (6K 965gm). 4. Mackerel, *Scomber scombrus*, 4lb 8dr (1K 828gm). 5. Pollack, *Pollachius pollachius*, 16lb (7K 257gm). 6. Thornback ray, *Raja clavata*, 21lb (9K 525gm). 7. Wrasse, ballan *Labrus bergylta*, 8lb 6oz 6dr (3K 808gm). All weights given are current records.

rock fishing should not prove rewarding. Usually the variety of fish differs considerably from the average sand and shingle coastline, and the methods which can be used provide a challenging alternative.

Rock fishing is, more often than not, a summer sport, as much as our rocky coastline is exposed to what can prove to be a succession of winter storms. Also, a number of species which often give sport around rocks leave inshore waters during winter. Remember that fish only frequent areas which hold reasonable supplies of food, and there are few places which offer less chances of rich feeding than a stretch of granite rocks being swept by storm-driven seas.

When spring arrives, and with it the annual miracle of the creation of life under the warming influence of the sun, all manner of changes occur. The sea blooms and small fish start shoaling, larger fish move in to feed on the smaller ones, and so the cycle unfolds.

In the main, those species which the angler will hunt are predators. The staple food of pollack, coalfish, conger and ling is other fish. Mackerel eat plankton and small fish, while wrasse gulp down crabs, prawns and bi-valves (such as mussels) which they find in beds of kelp, another feature of a rocky coastline.

Sometimes there are patches of clear sand or gravel close to rocks, and these areas may yield ray, dogfish and even turbot and brill. Where these conditions exist, use standard leger or paternoster tackle, and baits such as strips cut from a fresh mackerel, squid or worm. This basic tackle is similar to standard beach angling equipment, but the other species such as pollack, ling, mackerel and, of course, bass will all snap at moving baits, so spinning tactics will catch all these species. One of the most effective lures is the famous West Country 'red-gill', an imitation sand eel which has been responsible for taking some memorable catches.

Other lures which can yield good results include various Must-lures' such as Koster, Toby, Egon and Krill. These sea lures can weigh as little as an ounce (28gm) but generally one about 2oz (60gm) will be more efficient. Use the sink and draw method, fishing as close to the sea bed as possible for ling (cod will also take these lures), but offer the bait higher for both pollack and coalfish. Bass might be taken at any depth.

Mackerel and garfish will take a spinner, and fishing for them with a medium rod and a blade spinner or a small silver Toby can be enormous fun. Float fishing is an ideal style and, in the long run, probably the most effective all-round method. Of the various styles of sea angling floats, I prefer the cigar-shaped variety for this situation. When correctly weighted it offers the least resistance to the fish. After it is set up and carrying the bait I like to see the float about three-quarters submerged.

Sharp rocks, and fish with equally sharp teeth, can sever nylon line, so incorporate about three feet of nylon-covered steel trace into the terminal rig. Use it from the hook up to a buckle or some kind of quick-release link.

There are several types of lead weight that perform adequately, but a barrel lead is as efficient as any. Place this on the line above the link, and stop the float rising by fixing a valve rubber at the appropriate place on the reel line. It can be an advantage to place a bead on the line between the float and the stop. This acts as a cushion and prevents the rubber stop from running through the line channel in the float.

It is impossible to be dogmatic about line strengths, but when angling for wrasse I would not generally use tackle exceeding 20lb BS. Hooks should be suited to the baits, but I have never found it necessary to use one larger than 2/0. Wrasse are frequently caught on a bait presented either above or alongside weed beds, and baits include worm, mussel, limpet and crab. They are strong creatures and although on average the fish you catch may not exceed 3 to 4lb they can give some excellent sport. When hooked a wrasse dives for cover, and once a fish gets into a thick bed of kelp you may well lose it. Draw the hooked fish from cover as soon as possible. Every so often take the line through a pad impregnated with a floatant, such as Mucillin. This will keep it on the surface and make striking a great deal easier.

Pollack, ling and coalfish are caught in a similar way, but it may be necessary to present the bait at various depths before the fish are contacted. Fish baits are generally more acceptable to these predators and a cluster of sand eels is excellent. These are available, frozen, from many tackle shops, and can be hooked either through the head or body. Several sprats offered in a similar way are very effective, but the head of a freshly caught mackerel, complete with entrails, is probably the most deadly of all. Push the hook through the eye sockets. When considering baits for sea fish, remember that the scent of blood is highly attractive to predators.

Conger also live amongst rocks, but usually in more sheltered regions as they are recognised as an all-the-year-round resident. An area which becomes barren for perhaps half the year would not attract conger, as they feed mainly on other fish. Float tackle using a half mackerel bait, fished on a size 4/0 or 5/0 hook and presented on or very close to the bed, is one way, but a paternoster or leger would be preferable if the sea bed conditions allowed either to be used.

When fishing for conger, use a considerably heavier line of 50 to 70lb BS, depending on the size of fish that can reasonably be expected. I prefer a braided line because it has no stretch, and this helps to keep the fish under more direct control. A steel trace to the hook is essential, and as fishing where there are plenty of snags can prove expensive, either use an expendable weight – such as a section of cycle innertube filled with wet sand – or attach the lead with a length of line of a much lower BS than the remainder of the tackle.

Conger possess steel-like strength, and the power of a large one has to be experienced to be believed. Despite this, they can be very timid when it comes to taking a bait. The first 'knock' or two will almost certainly be quite gentle. At this point give the fish some slack line and, with any luck, this will be drawn slowly out. As the run develops, give it time to get the bait well and truly into its mouth and then strike – and strike hard. Never be in a hurry to set the hook. The fish can make several false moves before deciding to take the bait properly. It is also always possible that another species, such as bass, will take a conger bait. So always be prepared for the unexpected.

Once the hook is set, the fish will do its best to back off into a fissure or get its body around a holdfast. If it succeeds, the angler will probably lose. So as soon as the hook is set, get the fish up off the bottom and into clear water. Conger shake their heads, spin and generally conduct a rough and rugged battle, but they seldom try to swim far. It is more of a stand-up slugging match. Play the fish right out until it can be drawn close enough to be gaffed.

When rock fishing always pay great attention to the problems of landing whatever you catch. Never expect to use your tackle as a crane. You will probably lose more fish than you get ashore if you do. It is absolutely essential that your foothold is secure. Never try landing a fish while standing on a sloping, weed-covered rock. The dangers are obvious. Never attempt to land a large fish by yourself. Leave it to your companion, and do not expect him to perform the impossible, or do anything stupidly dangerous.

When the fish is thoroughly beaten, and not before, draw it to within easy gaffing or netting distance and then perform the operation in one easy movement. Bring the fish up onto the ledge, take it well clear of the edge, unclip the hook trace and kill the fish immediately.

Boat fishing

Although boat fishing opens up a whole new vista of sporting opportunities, it also means the angler must completely reassess his attitude to safety. The *Seaway Code,* an excellent booklet on the subject, is available free from Harbour Masters, HM Coastguard, yacht and many sea angling clubs, as well as through public libraries.

Never overload your craft. For practical fishing purposes, assume that a 10ft dinghy is suitable for one, and for each additional person you need another 2ft of craft. An efficient anchor of the correct weight must be carried (about 1lb for every foot of boat) and although relatively thin lines can be strong enough to hold the boat at anchor, you need a bulky rope to haul the anchor up. Thin line will cut into your hands, but a 2in-diameter rope will be far easier to use.

Learn how to carry out simple checks and running repairs to your engine, and never go to sea without an ample supply of fuel. All dinghies should also carry oars and rowlocks which fit properly and are secured to the boat.

Never go to sea without flares and/or distress rockets, and all those on board must have efficient life-jackets, not just buoyancy aids. Use jackets which conform to BSS. Store the flares and rockets in a waterproof container, and keep them where they will not spill even if the boat capsizes. Make sure that you could still reach them if you were holding onto the upturned craft. In the event of a capsize, stay with the boat.

Never try hauling the anchor over any part of the craft except the bows. Hauling in over the side can easily cause the boat to tip and fill with water. Keep a careful check on the weather, and remember that a stiff breeze blowing with the tide run produces relatively small waves. However, wind over tide creates a very lumpy situation in a short space of time, and a long push back home in these conditions can be hazardous.

In short, always consult the local Coastguard before you go out if there is any doubt about the conditions. Always leave word with a reliable person ashore, telling them the direction you are taking and the time you expect to be back, and make sure you return on time. While at sea, never ignore anyone who appears to have problems. In fact it is always preferable to fish in company with at least one other boat and crew rather than play a lone hand.

Another safety aspect concerns the fish you catch and the tackle being used. Keep the bottom boards clear of both fish and slime: the dangers are obvious. Take great care with your tackle, keeping anything not in use stowed away and never stand up in a small boat when playing a fish, nor when netting or gaffing it.

Although there are a number of species which are more commonly associated with boat fishing, there is, of course, a considerable overlap in many areas. It is frequently easier for the boat angler to use tidal currents as a means of imparting movement to the bait, so techniques can differ. For example, the boat can be set on a long drift over sand and mud where a bottom-fished bait could attract flounders and plaice. Similar tactics over broken ground might yield whiting or cod. Bream can be caught by anchoring over a hard chalk bed or close to clumps of rock or rough ground, and then letting the current draw the bait so that it is fished in a series of hops over the bed. In common with other styles of angling, both the changing seasons, temperature and the underwater environment are, in general, the factors which decide what you will catch.

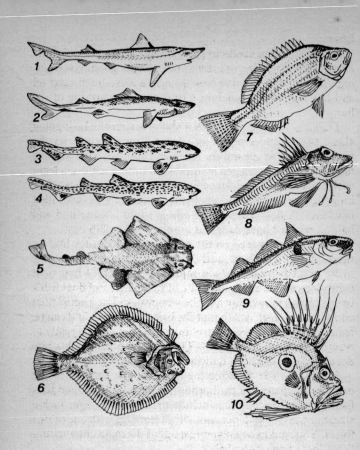

1. Tope, Galeorhinus galeus, 74lb 11oz 33K 876gm. 2. Spur-
dog, Squalus acanthias, 21lb 3oz 7dr 9K 622gm. 3. Bull huss,
Scyliorhinus stellaris, 21lb 3oz 9K 610gm. 4. Dogfish (lesser spot-
ted), Scyliorhinus canicular, 4lb 1oz 13dr 1K 865gm. 5.
Monkfish, Squatina squatina, 66lb 29K 936gm. 6. Turbot,
Scophthalmus maximus, 32lb 3oz 14K 599gm. 7. Bream
(black), Spondyliosoma cantharus, 6lb 14oz 4dr 3K 125gm. 8.
Gurnard (Red), Aspitrigla cuculus, 5lb 2K 268gm. 9. Haddock,
Melanogramnius aeglefinus, 13lb 11oz 4dr 6K 215gm. 10. John
Dory, Zeus faber, 11lb 14oz 5K 386gm.

Bass

Offshore reefs and sandbars, and shingle and sandbars at the entrance to a harbour or estuary often make good bass hunting grounds. Use the tide flow to carry a loose-lined sand eel and fish from a boat anchored in deep water up-tide of the bar.

Trail a sand eel spinner or bar spoon astern of a boat going ahead slowly under power or, if conditions permit, let the boat drift over or around the mark and spinfish with suitable tackle. Where the sea bed is suitable, wander tackle or a leger with a two-hook trace can be fished from a drifting boat. Use king rag, soft crab or the head and entrails of a freshly killed mackerel. A float fished small whole squid is a method and bait on which I have caught a number of 6 to 8lb bass.

Bass frequently feed on the various creatures they find on the stones of a harbour wall or jetty. These small creatures make good baits, as do shrimps and prawns. When tidal conditions allow, anchor up-tide of the mark, and float fish a bait such as a prawn down to the stonework. Use a small float and a minimum of lead so that the bait streams out and can be fished with care. Keep control over the line, and be ready to react to a sudden strong pull. The float is not so much a bite detector as a marker to indicate the position of the bait.

A bank of rocks flanking the entrance to a harbour or the deep water channel at the harbour mouth are both good bass fishing areas. Tactics can include drifting with leger tackle streaming astern and, occasionally, a leger rig with one or two flyers. You could also anchor just out of the main channel and fish a loose line or spinfish.

When using dead sand eels as bait, you may find that the fish are biting short and leaving the eel head on the hook. When this happens, use a baiting needle to draw the trace up through the eel, leaving the hook point protruding from the vent.

A hooked bass is a lively creature. Whilst playing it, keep the rod tip up and let it tire itself against the spring in the rod. Take care when netting. It is best to leave it to your companion who should sink the net, whilst you play the fish over it and then lift the net swiftly and cleanly. As soon as the fish is in the boat, despatch it with a sharp blow from a priest. However, always return bass less than 15in long.

Bream

Bream are a wonderfully sporting species, but they have been grossly overfished. Unfortunately, the best of the sport occurs at the very time the shoals are massed for spawning, so for the sake not only of the species but also of those anglers yet to come, always return a proportion of your catch.

Fish a moving bait and, ideally, use tackle as light as possible. When fishing from an anchored boat, present the bait in a series of jumps or hops. Let the line pay out until the lead strikes bottom. Check the outflow and let the tide lift the tackle several feet, then pay out more line. Repeat this action until the pressure of water on the line makes it impossible to control the tackle correctly.

There is no set tackle arrangement. Try a leger with a 3 to 6ft trace from weight to hook, or a paternoster with a trace of similar length fixed to the line a foot or so above the weight. When fishing a trace this long, twisting is often a problem. An anti-kink vane fixed half-way should cure it.

Successful bream fishing hinges on three main factors: local knowledge of the marks (as the fish are not widespread when shoaled up for spawning); the ability to manipulate the light tackle and balance the weight of lead against the pull of the tide; and the judicious use of groundbait.

There are occasions when 4 or 6oz of lead, a 20lb BS line and a matching boat rod are necessary because the tidal condition would defeat lighter equipment. However, for me, bream fishing means no more than a 2oz weight, 10lb BS line and a spinning or light casting rod.

It is sometimes possible to use a lighter line than one might imagine. The greater diameter of a heavier line offers more resistance than a lighter one, so to some extent one is caught up in a spiral. The heavier the line the more lead there is needed to get the tackle down and the larger the weight the heavier the line needs to be to hold it.

Throughout the cycle of one tide it can be necessary to change leads quite often as the flow increases and slackens.

Remember the importance of fishing a moving bait, and the fact that the fish will often be further from the bed during the slack water periods, when sliding float gear will catch them. Take into consideration, too, the position of your boat. If you are catching fish during the ebb and nothing on the flood, it could be that you have swung away from the mark and your bait is far from where it should be. Bream can be shoaled up in a relatively small area.

A variety of baits will tempt bream but I have found that lug worm, strips of squid with a mussel on the tip, hermit crab and fresh mackerel are the most effective. When baiting with fresh mussel, tip the hook with a small piece of squid or the tail-end of a worm. This will hold the soft mussel bait in position.

The bream's mouth is a relatively small one, so use a hook and baits to match. A size 1 or 2 is frequently large enough but err on the small size, particularly if fishing in very clear water. Under these conditions, the further away from the boat you can work your bait the more successful you are likely to be. A bream bite is very definite. If you are fishing correctly and keeping the tackle under control, it should not be necessary to do more than just tighten the line to hook your quarry.

Without doubt, groundbaiting helps enormously, and it can be done in several ways. The most efficient requires an open-weave sack or a large square of small mesh net. Use minced fish offal and bran, plus pilchard oil. Place a large stone (an old house brick will do) into the bottom of the sack, fill it with groundbait and lower it to the bottom. Then bring it up two or three feet so that the tide just washes the bait away. Watch the tide level constantly, and make the necessary adjustments according to whether the tide is rising or falling. Some anglers use a mixture of cooked grains and grit mixed roughly in equal parts (volume, not weight), but with costs as they are, I find it difficult to justify using such commodities as wheat and rice.

Bream are splendid fighters and, taken on light tackle, they provide memorable sport. They should be netted when brought to the surface – light rods are not built to be used as cranes. When unhooking bream, remember that, in common with bass, they have very sharp spines on their dorsal fin. Hold them in a cloth and grasp from under the body. This will save you from a painful wound.

Conger

All that has been said about conger when rock fishing applies equally to boat fishing. But deepwater offshore marks are more likely to provide the really big fish weighing up to 100lb, so much stronger tackle is advisable.

Rods matched to 60 or 70lb BS line are not out of place, and size 10/0 hooks baited with whole fish weighing perhaps 1½lb are the scale of things when fishing for really big conger. Never forget to use a steel trace as the conger's teeth will slice through nylon.

One word of warning: this is not a pastime to be undertaken by anglers fishing from a 12ft dinghy. A conger of 70 or 80lb would prove a very dangerous creature on board such a small craft. If one is taken, play it right out. Bring it to the surface and then secure it with a large hook fixed to a length of strong line or light rope. Get the creature's head out of the water and secure the line to the Sampson post at the bow, or bring the line in over the anchor fair-lead and tie-off inboard. Take the conger ashore in this position and do not attempt to get it on-board. If the fish is alive, you are only courting disaster as they are immensely powerful creatures.

Conger is very good to eat. Take cutlets from the body starting just behind the gills. It does tend to get bony as you get towards the tail. Boiled or steamed and served with parsley sauce it's delicious.

Dogfish

This general title covers a number of species which all belong to the Selachii class of cartilaginous fishes, as distinct from the bony fishes, such as bream, cod and conger. Dogfish, shark, monkfish, ray and skate are all in this class, and the various species range in size from the relatively small lesser spotted dogfish of around 1lb 8oz to the 500lb Mako shark.

From the sporting standpoint, only the greater spotted

(bull huss or nurse hound) and the spur-dog, are worth mentioning in this group. Even these are only half-hearted in their approach to a fight, unless conditions allow the use of light tackle.

Catching them is not difficult. Use orthodox leger tackle with hook sizes 2/0 to 4/0 fixed to a short, yard-long wire trace and use fish, mussel and squid for bait. The short boat-fishing rods associated with this style of sea angling must be matched to the conditions prevailing in the particular area.

Local knowledge is necessary to find the marks which hold dogfish, but generally they move in packs a fair distance offshore, feeding greedily on the various animals living on or in the sea bed. Spur-dog hunt other fish such as mackerel and herring. Both the lesser and greater spotted dogfish are unpleasant creatures to unhook. Their skin is exceptionally rough and they wind their sinuous body around the hand and arm holding them, an action which can draw blood. As soon as the fish is on board, stun it before attempting to remove the hook with a pair of pliers or forceps.

Spur-dog have two dorsal fins and at the leading edge there is a very sharp spine which can penetrate even a rubber boot if the fish is stepped on. If your skin is pierced by one of these spines, clean the wound and get medical advice as soon as possible.

Both the lesser and greater spotted dogfish make reasonable eating, but they must be skinned first, and for this task you must have a very sharp knife, a pair of pliers and a large piece of clean cloth. Gut and thoroughly clean (do not remove the head) and then trim the fins level with the body. Using just the tip of the knife, cut around the collar, just breaking the skin and not cutting into the flesh. Make a similar cut, only skin deep, from the collar to the tail, following a line along the top of the back, and finally make another cut from the belly opening to the tail.

Using the tip of the knife, lift a small flap of skin at the point where the incision around the collar joins the score line down the back, wrap the cloth around the head, grasp the head in one hand and the flap of skin with the pliers and just pull. If the skin has been cut correctly, it will strip down the body from head to tail quite easily. When both sides have been dealt with, remove the head. The body can be cut into chunks and cooked in a variety of ways from deep fried in batter, to being baked in cream and seasoning, with the addition of parmesan cheese.

Smaller spur-dog make fair eating, but the larger specimens tend to have a strong flavour. It is sometimes sold as 'flake', the name used by the trade.

When conditions are suitable for float fishing, spur-dog can be taken in this way, and on light tackle such as a heavy spinning rod, they can give quite a reasonable account of themselves. Use a sliding float rig set to present the bait about 3 to 6ft off the bottom.

Flounder

Boat angling for flounders is an interesting sport as it can be done in a variety of ways. The best is trolling a baited spoon. Use king rag as bait, row and keep your craft going ahead slightly faster than the tide flow. Make sure the oars are attached by line to your boat, then they won't go overboard whilst you are landing the fish. Wander tackle, which has its origins in commercial fishing, is also efficient.

Float and spoon fishing is practised in many areas, particularly in the central southern regions, and during the summer and autumn period when crabs are troublesome, it's a good way to keep the bait out of their reach.

Gurnard

There are four varieties of these odd-looking creatures, which the boat angler may catch while bottom fishing over sandy or muddy ground. The grey gurnard is the most widespread, reaching a size of just over 2lb, and its flesh is excellent. Cut a fillet from both flanks, but beware of its various spines and jagged edges. There is a lot of waste but, for all that, the flesh is worth the trouble of preparing.

Tub gurnard weigh up to 11lb or more and the flesh is good to eat. They are also plentiful.

The red gurnard is a medium-size fish in the range, up to

about 5lb, but the streaked gurnard is really of little account, seldom caught weighing more than 12oz to 1lb. Gurnard will take fish, worm and similar baits.

Haddock

This is a popular species which tends to have a fairly localised distribution in various parts of the British Isles. They are mainly bottom feeders but will often take a bait two or three feet up. Try leger tackle with two flyers, size 1/0 and 2/0 and Norwegian sea spoons baited with mussels, clams, lugworm, strips of mackerel or herring – the fresher the bait the better.

Haddock fight well, and if conditions permit use light-to-medium tackle but do not try to bully the fish. They will dive for cover if possible and shake their whole bodies in an attempt to shed the hook.

Drift fishing is often the most productive. When using this method over broken ground keep the rod working so that the lead weight is just striking the bottom and not dragging over it as this will result in a fair amount of lost tackle.

John Dory

This is one of the best tasting fish in the sea, but they tend to be caught more by accident than design. The John Dory is a strange looking creature, reminiscent of an oval dinner-plate standing on edge.

They are taken on both leger and paternoster rigs and they feed mainly on small fish. Because they are solitary creatures, if you catch one you may wait a year or ten before taking another. A John Dory of 3 or 4lb can be considered exceptional.

Ling

The largest of this species are normally taken from around wrecks and reefs some 20 fathoms or more deep. Some of the finest marks are off Devon and Cornwall, over some wrecks in parts of the North Sea and off the Scottish coast. Ling weighing 30 and 40 lb are not uncommon in these areas, and a whole mackerel mounted on a pirk fixed to a steel wire trace is suitable terminal tackle.

Score the bait's body to release the juices and lower to the bottom, and then bring it up a way so that you reduce the chances of snagging the bed. A heavy pirk (perhaps 1lb or more) in deep water is kept under better control – and certainly striking is more definite – if a braided or wire line is used.

Ling dive for cover as soon as they have taken the bait and they must be held away from the rocks if you are to win. They are immensely powerful fish and demand the use of really heavy tackle. This sport is mainly undertaken from professional charter boats, many of which will hire suitable equipment.

Monkfish – ray and skate

These species frequent muddy and sandy areas and, without exception, leger tackle is the method. Always use a steel wire trace as they have teeth capable of severing nylon. Monkfish are relatively scarce in most parts, while thornback ray are probably the most common.

Depending on the size of fish one can reasonably expect to catch, hook sizes and tackle range from medium rods and 30lb BS line with 3/0 to 4/0 hooks up to the heaviest of tackle. 10/0 hooks baited with 1lb fillets are needed when fishing with 100lb-plus skate in mind.

Skate and ray frequently take the bait rather furtively. They usually 'flop' onto it and may take it completely before starting to edge away, drawing line very slowly. This slow take is most characteristic of these fish. Give them time, but as the run develops and becomes definite, strike hard to drive the hook well home.

Both monkfish and skate, can then pose the angler with a variety of problems. For example, a large monk can move away with a surprising turn of speed, and its powerful run can take some stopping. Get it up off the bottom as quickly as possible, and be prepared for the fish to dive strongly as you bring it to the surface for the first time.

Although a fairly sporting fish, monk have little else to commend them as the flesh is too rough and rank to eat. Small skate and ray up to 16lb make good eating, but large ones are tough.

Both ray and skate of this size fight well, but beware of their habit of diving hard when first brought to the surface, and keep your fingers well clear of their teeth. Monkfish, skate and ray have very powerful jaw muscles and teeth designed for crushing and grinding. A large skate can crush a lobster, so what chance would fingers stand? The stingray, mentioned earlier, is also caught by boat anglers, but probably the most common species of ray is the thornback, named because of the rose-like thorns on its back. They are sharp and capable of inflicting very painful wounds. Use a gaff to boat these fish. Release the hook trace and kill the fish before attempting to remove the hook.

Professional 'pot' fishermen will always use the unwanted carcasses for lobster bait, but for human beings, only the 'wings' are worth eating. Cut these away and skin with a sharp, thin-bladed knife. It is also possible to just lift a corner of skin and then strip with a pair of pliers, but this skill needs practice.

Pollack

The best of the sport with these fish is found a long way offshore over wreck and reefs in very deep water. Such marks abound with 15 and 20lb fish, and they can be caught on baited pirks, artificial eels such as the famous Red Gill, as well as on strips of mackerel and herring.

Use strong tackle and a paternoster rig with a 10 or 12ft wire trace broken by one or two swivels, or perhaps a two-hook leger rig. Keep the bait moving, and as soon as the fish is on, draw it away from cover as they will dive immediately and probably slice your line on a jagged rock.

As with the best of ling fishing, it is mainly a sport associated with professionally-manned charter boats.

Tope

These are caught mainly on leger tackle, using a 6 to 8ft 50lb BS nylon-covered steel wire trace. The weight is carried on a Clements quick-release sliding boom, or a Kilmore which is stopped with a matchstick or section of rubber band to give an extra 10 or maybe 20ft of line between weight and bait.

A long trace has a two-fold purpose. Firstly, it allows the tope, a curiously careful creature, to inspect the bait with a minimum chance of it feeling the restrictions of the lead weight and, secondly, tope frequently roll the trace around their body. Ordinary nylon will fray when rubbed against their extremely rough hide, the initial 6–8ft of nylon-covered steel will take the chafing.

The nylon-covered steel section should have one swivel, preferably two. Make sure that your reel carries a minimum of 300 yards of line, as a large tope can take a 100 yards or more on its first run. If your bait is 40 or 50 yards astern of your anchored craft, you haven't a lot to bargain with if the fish is very lively.

Where skate and ray will lay on the bottom where their bodies create an almost suction-like effect, tope will tear away down-tide, change direction suddenly, boil up to the surface and then dive just as quickly. In shallow water they may even leap clear, a most electrifying sight. Tope are mainly caught over sand, mud and shingle beds, and especially where there is a good tide race.

Baits range from a whole side of mackerel, to a whole fish cut slantways across its body, the head and entrails forming one bait, the tail section another. A mackerel head can be hooked through the eye sockets which provide a good hold-fast for the hook. Use hooks to match the size of bait. Usually this means something between a 4/0 to 6/0. Make sure the hook tip is not masked by the bait, and always wait for the second run to start before striking.

As striking a tope can be a long-range job, I prefer to use a braided line (30 to 35lb BS) which provides a more definite action.

Although tope are mainly a summer and autumn species, some are caught in British waters throughout the year. Large females often come relatively close inshore during the late spring and early summer to give birth to live young. A female caught at this time of year may give birth to young after she has been boated. Sometimes the young will survive if released immediately.

When the hooked fish is played right out, draw it alongside. With care, it is possible to lift the fish from the water by grasping its dorsal fin with one hand and the wrist with the other.

Two anglers working in unison can operate this scheme quite simply, but the angler handling the fish must give all the instructions. You cannot have two issuing orders. Lift the fish inboard, release the trace, place the rod to one side and then pinion the fish with one hand grasping its tail, the other its dorsal fin. Hold the fish still while the other removes the hook with a pair of pliers.

Protect your hands by wearing a pair of leather-palmed gloves and keep a knob of wood between its teeth while taking the hook out. Handle the fish firmly but with care and put it back into the sea as soon as possible. There is little point in killing a fish that is not worth eating.

This is not an operation for a small dinghy, and serious tope fishing should not be attempted from 10 to 12ft craft, as hooking a really large fish can be hazardous.

Float fishing for tope is an interesting method, but conditions are seldom suitable. Use a sliding float rig, bait a 6/0 hook with a whole squid or cuttle head, and let it drift away from the boat. Set the tackle to fish the bait at about three-quarters depth. Never be in a hurry to strike, but if you do hit the fish too soon and it drops the bait, do not reel in immediately. The tope may well return after a few minutes. Never wait too long as the fish may have stripped the bait and left you with a bare hook.

One of the biggest problems of specialised tope fishing is bait presentation. These fish are frequently found in an area providing a really fast tide race and this can spin a bait, causing the trace to kink. Make sure the swivels are working correctly, and use what might be described as a 'streamlined bait' in really fast tide runs. Groundbaiting is a help, as tope, in common with all members of the shark tribe, have an acute sense of smell.

Whiting
These are a very popular species, and are sometimes referred

to as silver whiting or, in the south, channel whiting. Fish of around 2lb can be considered a fair size. They are normally found in shoals, over sand, mud and shingle, where they feed on other fish, shrimps, crabs and worms.

Fish a leger rig with two flyers, or orthodox paternoster tackle with nylon traces about 1½ to 2ft long. Use size 1/0 or 2/0 hooks and bait with mussel, strips of fish, cuttle or small whole squid. These fish are attracted by movement, and all the best catches of whiting that I have made have come to baits fished in much the same way as for bream fishing.

Groundbaiting also helps to attract these fish, which will group them astern of your craft. Where the sea bed is relatively snag free, fishing a paternoster while drifting can bring excellent results.

Chapter 6

Where to fish

Coarse fishing

For all practical purposes, the best coarse angling waters throughout England and Wales are controlled either by clubs or associations, bodies such as Regional Water Authorities, companies specialising in providing leisure facilities, or private individuals.

British Waterways Board, the National Trust and the Forestry Commission control some waters. Contact either the national headquarters of these organisations in London, or the regional or local offices.

The occasional or holiday angler will almost certainly be best served by contacting the Fisheries Department of the appropriate RWA and asking for a copy of their angling guide. RWA angling guides will certainly give the angler all the relevant local information that is necessary about the available water, as well as up-to-date details of the various bye-laws and rod licence charges.

In both Scotland and Ireland, there is a vast amount of coarse fishing which is either entirely free or virtually so, but always check with the landowner before starting to fish. *Never* assume angling is free. The prolific waters of Fermanagh, Cavan and many other parts of Ireland have produced many legendary catches in the past, and will do so again in the future. Both the Ulster Tourist Board and Irish Tourist Board issue excellent coarse angling guides, and useful data about Scottish coarse angling can be obtained from the Perth and Central Highlands Tourist Association in

Perth and the South West Scotland Tourist Association at the Town Hall, Lochmaben, Dumfrieshire. The Lochmaben area is probably the most organised of all Scottish areas when it comes to coarse angling.

Game fishing

Throughout England and Wales the Water Authorities probably control the bulk of the trout fishing which is available to the general public on a day-ticket basis.

There are many reservoirs which have established enviable reputations for the quality of their trout fishing. Bewl Bridge, Chew Magna, Blagdon, Fewston, Thruscross, Wimbleball and Upper Tamar are just a few picked at random from an area stretching from Cornwall to East Sussex, north to Yorkshire and back to the West Country, near Bristol. These and many similar waters are well stocked and produce fish up to 7lb and more.

There are also a variety of hotels and pubs as well as private individuals, clubs and associations which offer trout fishing, sometimes on a day-ticket basis or possibly for longer periods. Once again the RWA fishery guides usually offer excellent coverage of such facilities.

Tourist boards, especially the Scottish, Irish, Ulster and Welsh, are also valuable sources of information on both trout and salmon fishing. Salmon fishing is strictly preserved, and all the previous recommendations about RWA and Tourist Boards applies most especially to this branch of angling.

Sea angling

There are many first-class sea angling centres around the British Isles and Eire, and the following information is really no more than an indication of the variety which is offered.

Along the south coast there are excellent facilities at many ports and resorts from Ramsgate to Falmouth, and also at places on the Channel Isles. Winter cod and whiting fishing around the south-east corner can be extremely good from both shore and boat, and at Dover the breakwater provides an excellent mark. The Dungeness shoreline, although bleak and exposed, still yields some worthwhile catches, even in these days of general scarcity.

At Eastbourne the local inshore fishermen offer some facilities for the boat-fishing enthusiast, and of course at nearby Newhaven there is an extensive charter-boat fleet. At the new Brighton Marina, there are charter boats and the nearby beaches are worth fishing, but also the harbour walls offer the angler some excellent sea angling opportunities. Littlehampton is another good charter-boat centre, and quite a number of similar ventures operate from Langstone and Portsmouth harbours.

The Needles area at the western tip of the Isle of Wight is fished by charter boats out of Poole and Lymington and, of course, the Dorset shoreline is a favourite with many beach anglers. Bass, flounders, plaice and various other species are caught hereabouts, but beware of the cliffs in this area as they can crumble and fall without warning.

Weymouth is another excellent centre. Boat anglers are well catered for and the Chesil Beach attracts many species, and occasionally yields some splendid catches. Here, as elsewhere, shore fishing has declined in recent years as a result of the many evils which beset sea fishing as a whole.

Travelling westwards, there is Brixham, Plymouth, Looe, Fowey, Mevagissey and Falmouth, all famous names which conjure visions of giant fish and spectacular catches.

Species such as pollack, wrasse, mackerel, garfish and bass are taken from a multitude of shore marks from Whitsand Bay to the Lizard and beyond. Always bear in mind the dangers associated with fishing from rocks exposed to hundreds of miles of open sea.

Offshore West Country marks such as the Eddystone reef, East and West Rutts, the Manacles and many others produce ling, conger, shark, pollack as well as small but still hard-fighting species such as red and black bream, haddock and, of course, mackerel, a much underrated sporting fish.

The Isle of Scilly is as yet a much underfished area, but it's not a place for the novice, nor for the person who would ignore local advice. These are rich waters, but they can also be exceedingly dangerous for those without a lot of local knowledge.

Along the north Cornish coast there are centres such as Newquay and Padstow and many shore marks such as Trevose Head which can offer good sport. This is an exposed stretch of shoreline, so take both care and as much local advice as you can get.

There are plenty of good sporting opportunities along the Welsh coastline, but probably the most organised boat angling centres include Conway, Rhyl and Aberystwyth, with towns such as Holyhead, Abersoch, Aberdovey and Saundersfoot providing excellent but somewhat limited services. Shore fishing around Wales is also good, particularly along the Pembrokeshire coastline and Cardigan Bay.

Access to parts of the north-east coast is difficult, but south-west Scotland has great potential. Much of the Scottish coastline is difficult to approach, as vast stretches are wild and desolate. But there are great opportunities opening up, and centres such as Ullapool and Thurso are charting a course which possibly others will follow.

Moving south down the east coast, there are a number of centres such as Whitby and Scarborough where boatmen cater for sea anglers looking for sport with fish such as codling. This coastline also offers ray, dabs and a variety of other species, and some would claim that the waters off the Yorkshire coastline can offer general sport which is second to none.

The Wash and parts of the coastline of East Anglia is also difficult to approach, but shore anglers catch a variety of species ranging from bass to cod, as well as flounders, eels, ray and whiting. Boat angling facilities exist at King's Lynn, Sheringham, Wells, Gorleston and Lowestoft and this area also boasts several piers which provide sport. There is Wellington pier at Great Yarmouth, Clacton Pier and two at Lowestoft.

Ireland is a mecca for both shore and boat anglers. There are great centres at Cork and Kinsale, as well as Fennit and Port Stewart. At Strangford Lough, a huge area just waiting for exploration, there are opportunities galore. Shore fishing at marks such as the Dingle area can still be exceptional, and the catches made along the Causeway coast are second to none.

All in all, for those who would venture a little and who are prepared to put effort and enthusiasm into their angling excursions, there is still much excitement and first-class sport to be found in the waters surrounding and contained in the British Isles.

Sea angling organisations

Bass Anglers Sport Fishing Society
J. Churchouse, 'Rishon', Longfield Road, Weymouth, Dorset.

British Conger Club
R. H. J. Quest, 5 Hill Crest, Mannamead, Plymouth, Devon.

National Federation of Sea Anglers
R. W. Page, 26 Downsview Crescent, Uckfield, Sussex, TN22 1UB.

National Mullet Club
G. Green, 53 Dowlands Close, Bexhill-on-Sea, Sussex.

Shark Angling Club of Great Britain
B. Tudor, Jolly Sailors Inn, West Looe, Cornwall.

Sea Anglers Match Federation
A. Yates, 1 Pineham Bottom Cotts, Pineham, Dover, Kent.

Irish Federation of Sea Anglers
H. O'Rorke, 67 Windsor Drive, Monkstown, Co. Dublin.

Scottish Federation of Sea Anglers
Mrs. C. Watson, 8 Frederick Street, Edinburgh, EH2 2HB.

Welsh Federation of Sea Anglers
G. E. Jones, 34 Coveny Street, Splott, Cardiff, CF2 2NN.

It should always be remembered that a number of sea fish are protected by the various size limits set out in the Sea-Fishing Industry (Immature Sea Fish) Order. These limits are well publicised at local fishing centres and are subject to revision. However, anglers normally accept a wider range of size limits, and several large associations set their own limits which members are expected to recognise.

The following is a guide, but check and make yourself familiar with locally accepted size limits.

	in	lb		in	lb
Bass	15		Rockling	5	
Bream	12		(Bearded)	8	
Brill	15		Silver (eel)	15	
Bull Huss	23		Spur Dog	23	
Coalfish	12		Shark (Blue)		40
Cod	18		Shark (Mako)		40
Conger	28		Shark (Porbeagle)		40
Dab	8		Shark (Thresher)		40
Lesser Spotted			All Skates (Long		
Dogfish	18		Nose, Common,		
Flounder	11		White)		5
Garfish	15		Ray (Thornback)		5
Gurnard	9		Ray (Blonde)		5
Haddock	14		Smoothound	20	
Hake	12		Sole	10	
Halibut		20	Sole (Lemon)	10	
John Dory	13		Scad	10	
Ling	28		Shad	10	
Mackerel	11		Tope		20
Megrim	10		Turbot	16	
Monkfish		15	Whiting	12	
Mullet	13		Witch	11½	
Plaice	10		Wrasse	9	
Pollack	12		Unclassified	8	
Pouting	10		All Other Rays		3

Other useful addresses:
National Anglers Council and The British Record (rod-caught) Fish Committee, P. H. Tombleson, 11 Cowgate, Peterborough, PE1 1LR.

Salmon and Trout Association
H. de W. Waller, Fishmongers' Hall, London, EC4R 9EL.